STAND UP PADDLING
Flatwater to Surf and Rivers

STAND UP PADDLING
Flatwater to Surf and Rivers

Rob Casey
Foreword by Dave Kalama

THE MOUNTAINEERS BOOKS

THE MOUNTAINEERS BOOKS
is the nonprofit publishing arm of The Mountaineers,
an organization founded in 1906 and dedicated to the exploration,
preservation, and enjoyment of outdoor and wilderness areas.

1001 SW Klickitat Way, Suite 201, Seattle, WA 98134

Distributed in the United Kingdom by Cordee, www.cordee.co.uk

Manufactured in the United States of America

Copy Editor: Colin Chisholm
Cover, book design, and layout: Peggy Egerdahl
Illustrator: Dennis Arneson
All photographs by author unless otherwise credited.
Photographs on pages 169–179 and 182–184 by Dan Gavare.
Cover photograph: *Tyler Hesse paddling his SUP on Puget Sound off Alki Point* © Rob Casey.
Frontispiece: *Paddler on Lake Washington during the 2009 Round the Rock SUP Race.*
Illustration on page 92 adapted from *Fundamentals of Kayak Navigation* by David Burch,
with permission of the author.

Library of Congress Cataloging-in-Publication Data
Casey, Rob.
  Stand up paddling : flatwater to surf and rivers / by Rob Casey.—1st ed.
    p. cm.
  Includes index.
  ISBN 978-1-59485-253-4 (pbk.)—ISBN 978-1-59485-325-8 (ebook)
  1. Sea kayaking. 2. Surfing. I. Title.
  GV788.5.C38 2011
  797.1'224—dc22
                          2010036807

♻ Printed on recycled paper

ISBN (paperback): 978-1-59485-253-4
ISBN (e-book): 978-1-59485-325-8

CONTENTS

CHAPTER 3

Flatwater Paddling

CHAPTER 4

Surfing

Preface

A few years ago I was paddling on Puget Sound near my home and saw my first stand up paddler. He seemed slow compared to my kayak, and it appeared to be a lot of work. That same year, after unsuccessfully trying a narrow, unstable stand up paddleboard (SUP) at a resort in Hawaii, I decided that the sport wasn't for me.

A year later, I noticed a second stand up paddler near my home. I decided to try a SUP again, but on a wider board, and this time I had a much better experience.

I had heard friends talk about the superior views from a SUP, and I began to see this for myself. Although I had sea kayaked for nearly a decade in this same part of Puget Sound, from my new higher perspective on the board I saw things I had never seen before. It was mesmerizing to paddle in 1–2 feet of clear water while watching the sandy bottom slowly drop into an abyss. The harbor seals that have followed me for years in my kayak could now be seen darting directly beneath my board. Another benefit was the ease with which I could slip off the board into the water to snorkel, or simply sit on the board with my feet in the water. I delighted in this newfound freedom.

Over time, I began to see other benefits as well, such as improved strength in my legs. I had heard of the benefits of stand up paddling to body core strength, and was now seeing results. My nagging lower back problem began to dissolve, and my balance and posture improved.

In time I learned to paddle my board so efficiently that I could keep up with my sea kayak friends while paddling our local waters, and I could surf with ease on the coast. I also felt closer to nature, with the water splashing up on my feet with every stroke. Although I still paddle my sea kayak sometimes, more often than not I prefer the SUP.

The author calls this "research." (Photo by Christy Cox)

Meanwhile, the sport has grown leaps and bounds. There are now three stand up paddling magazines, professional stand up paddlers, dozens of companies building boards and paddles, and even a TV show focused on the sport. Stand up paddling is so versatile that people are using SUPs on rivers, in surf, on long expeditions, in races, for fishing, and simply paddling around their home waters. As more and more people recognize the joys of this unique sport, stand up paddleboards are bound to become a common sight on waterways around the world.

ECOLOGICAL AWARENESS

Stand up paddling, by its very nature, will bring you into intimate contact with the natural world. You'll be crossing beaches, skimming over the water, and, like it or not, falling *in* the water. Respect these environments in every way you can: tread lightly; pick up trash; carry out whatever you bring with you; and be sensitive to the needs of wildlife.

Do not harass sea life, and stay clear of larger marine mammals, such as whales. Our curiosity about such animals also endangers them. I once saw a large sailboat approaching within a foot of a buoy in order to give the passengers closer photographs of California sea lions resting on it. In another incident, I came across a child with a harbor seal pup in his arms, posing for his mother's photograph.

As stewards of the environment, it is our responsibility to take care of the places where we live and play. If you see any kind of toxic spill, such as oil, report it. Join local clubs or groups that work to maintain and preserve your beaches and waterways.

A NOTE ABOUT SAFETY

Safety is an important concern in all outdoor activities. No book can alert you to every hazard or anticipate the limitations of every reader. The descriptions of techniques and procedures in this book are intended to provide general information. This is not a complete text on stand up paddling technique. Nothing substitutes for formal instruction, routine practice, and plenty of experience. When you follow any of the procedures described here, you assume responsibility for your own safety. Use this book as a general guide to further information.

—*The Mountaineers Books*

Acknowledgments

The following people and organizations were instrumental in helping me to write this book: Corran Addison, Imagine Surfboards; Patrick Aio; Elliott Almond; Candice Appleby; Bobby Arzadon, Perfect Wave Surf Shop; Bill Babcock; Brandi Baksic; John Beausang; Steve Boehne, Infinity Surfboards; David Burch, Starpath Publications; Fletcher Burton; Ken Campbell, Azimuth Expeditions; Krista Carlson; Dave Collins; Ken and Ellen DeBondt; Clay Feeter, Publisher, *Stand Up Paddle Journal*; Dan Gavere, professional stand up paddler; David Gimlett; Nikki Gregg, fitness professional; George and Barbara Gronseth, The Kayak Academy; Lars L.E. Hansen; Gregg Hoesterey; Ken Hoeve, Surftech; Dan Hogg; Reid Inouye, Publisher, *Stand Up Paddle Magazine*; Shawn Jennings; Dennis Judsen, Santa Cruz Surf Kayak Festival; David Kalama; Jennifer Kalmbach; Fox Lach, Managing Editor, *Stand Up Paddle Magazine;* Reg Lake; Paul Langer, Flow Paddleboards; Wade Lawson; Evan Lloyd, Tomahawk Boards; John Lull; Bob McDermott; William Mattos; Herbie and John Meyer, Northwest Outdoor Center, Seattle; Jim Miller, Werner Paddles; Andre Niemeyer; Chuck Patterson; David Schleifer; Vince Shay; Dave Shively, Jeff Moag, and Joe Carberry, *SUP Magazine;* Surf Ballard, Seattle; Tom Swetish; Todd Switzer; Calvin Tom, BoardFisher.com; Jeff Underwood and Dan Eberhardt, NW Paddle Surfers; Urban Surf, Seattle; Michael Vaughan; and Beau Whitehead.

I'd also like to thank and dedicate this book to my partner Christy Cox, who wrote the profiles that appear throughout the book, and to my parents.

Foreword

While it might seem like a new sport in your home waters, stand up paddling has been around for quite some time. The Peruvians can lay claim to the sport's origins with their "totora" reed paddle boats, ancient predecessors to our current boards. Another early boat-board hybrid was the Arabic "hasake," most likely used for fishing in the same way as the totora vessels.

But in my heart, I firmly believe that the Hawaiians were the ones to develop the sport that most closely relates to today's stand up paddling. And, no, Laird Hamilton and I are not the ones that created stand up, though perhaps you could say we helped turn the spotlight on this incredible sport. To really give credit where credit is due, however, I would start with Duke Kahanamoku and John Zapotocky. Most of us know that the Duke is considered the father of modern surfing; John Zapotocky was a gentleman from the mainland who found himself living in Waikiki. As the story goes, he saw the Duke doing stand up one day and decided that it looked like his type of surfing. The Duke was just using a standard canoe paddle; at the time, canoe paddles were much longer than they are now, though still not as long as today's SUP gear. As he watched, John thought that a longer rowboat oar would make the perfect paddle for the stand-up experience. So on one of his trips to the mainland he purchased several oak rowing oars. He went on to do stand up exclusively for many years but the sport never quite took off, in part because Duke, one of the greatest athletes and surfers at the time, was pushing hard to share prone-style surfing with the world instead.

Dave Kalama on a downwinder off Maui, Hawaii (Photo by Darryl Wong)

It's interesting that, while stand up paddling has been around in one form or another for ages, the stars have aligned only now in the 21st century to make it popular. Why? I think the general enthusiasm that people have to be outside is stronger these days. People want to be immersed in nature, commune with the elements, turn off electronic distractions, and get away from it all, if only for a little while.

I can only think of a couple of sports that offer the diversity that stand up provides. Cycling or some forms of boating may also offer the wide variety of applications you can find with stand up. Small wave riding, large wave riding, downwinders, rivers, channel crossings, flatwater, exploration paddling, racing, cruising, fishing, exercise—even taking the dog for a ride—it's all possible on a stand up paddle board. Whatever application attracts you to this sport, it uses the same ingredients: just a board and a paddle. It's amazing to me that two very common items can be combined to create endless possibilities for all of us to explore. That simple combination takes any body of water and transforms it into a playground or exercise gym or therapy for balancing our minds and bodies.

The first time you try standing on a board, it can feel like the relationship you've had with the earth, for however

Commune with the elements and your friends while stand up paddling.

many years, has just been shattered. You feel like a newborn moose trying to find its balance on wobbly legs. At least that's how a lot of us felt the first time we stood up! But very quickly your subconscious goes to work and, like the baby moose, you are on your feet and moving in no time.

In fact, one of the contributing factors to stand up's recent popularity is the ease with which you can enter the sport. Beginner boards are now so stable and user-friendly that success is within everyone's reach soon after starting. A protected bay or calm lake provides the first-timer with a very controlled situation that enables him or her to feel confident right from the start. Yet at the same time, the seasoned adrenaline junkie can get his or her fix, too: Try paddling to some outer reef on a 20- to 40-foot day and *not* come in buzzing from excitement. It's impossible! (But the river action some guys are doing now? Well, it's just plain crazy.) There is a level of SUP adventure that can accommodate everyone—as well as push you ever so gently toward your limits.

I've seen firsthand how this sport transforms 65-year-old men who felt their best days were behind them into frothing little grommets who can't wait to ride their next wave. You can see a renewed zest for life that only comes with true passion.

I've also seen 30-something women who have never gone more than knee-deep in the water paddle miles on their stand up boards. I've even seen some of the hardest-core surfers unwillingly allow themselves to become so addicted to SUP that they sell all their prone boards and only ride stand up boards now. While quite simple in its demeanor, this sport has a way of becoming so damn much fun it changes your perspective on things you know well, just enough to make them seem brand new again.

You can think of this book and author Rob Casey's instruction as a key of sorts. It will unlock a door of possibilities limited only by your imagination and personal goals. It will let you into a sport that connects you with people who have a robust passion for being. It's a key to feeling truly alive by simply getting your skin wet, and by enjoying a shared smile from a fellow paddler.

I hope that stand up paddling provides you with all of the fun and adventure with which it has blessed me, as well as the renewed health and fulfillment it allows me to experience on a daily basis.

Aloha,
Dave Kalama
Kula, Hawaii

History of Stand Up Paddling
by Corran Addison

Many people mistakenly believe that big wave surfers Laird Hamilton and Dave Kalama invented stand up paddling; however, the roots of the sport run much deeper. For 3,000 years Peruvian fishermen used a small, unstable reed-woven craft called a *caballitos de totora*. To propel the craft, the fisherman used a long bamboo shaft shaped like a kayak paddle. They would surf back to shore after a day of fishing. In Africa, warriors stood on dugout-type canoes called pirogues to silently approach enemy positions, using their spears as paddles.

In 1778, Captain James Cook sailed into the Hawaiian Islands and became the first European to witness the Hawaiian people surfing. The village chief had the biggest board, sometimes as big as 5 meters long, while the lesser villagers were content with smaller 2–3 meter boards. Hawaiian natives commonly paddled out and onto the waves. Surfboards and canoes were ritually carved from the Koa tree. *Hoe he'e nalu* is the Hawaiian phrase for stand up paddle surfing, while *he'e nalu* means surfing without a paddle.

In 1886, photographer Peter Henry Emerson captured a photo of a man stand up paddling through the marshes of England's East Anglia. Possibly the first photograph ever taken of the sport, the image is called "Quanting the Marsh Hay." A more commonly recognized incarnation of stand up paddling are the gondoliers of Venice, Italy, who actually use a paddle

Nikki Gregg and her dog, Nui, enjoy a calm paddle.

Quanting the Marsh Hay
(Photo by P.H. Emerson)

rather than a pole to propel the gondolas through the narrow canals of the city.

In Tel Aviv, Israel, lifeguards have been using a stand up board called a *hassakeh* since the first decades of the twentieth century, an idea borrowed from fishermen that dates back hundreds of years. Using a board almost 5 feet wide and a double-bladed paddle, the lifeguard can paddle quickly to a distressed person and haul him on board. The standing position gives the lifeguard a better vantage point. In the late 1930s, two Brazilian surfers, Osmar Goncalves and Joao Roberto Hafers, rode a stand up board called a *tabua havaiana* (Hawaiian plank), shaped by Julio Putz.

In the 1940s in Waikiki Beach, Hawaii, legendary surfer, lifeguard, and Olympian Duke Kahanamoku and surf instructor Leroy AhChoy would sometimes use paddles to help them stand on their boards to get a better view of the surfers in the water and of incoming swells. Occasionally they used the paddles to steer while surfing. Leroy's brother Bobby, injured in a car accident and unable to swim or even kneel, would paddle into the surf zone shouting hints to others with his cigarettes lashed to his arm and a camera around his neck. The two brothers also introduced the sport to their father, as well as to John Zapotocky, who is often credited as the father of modern stand up paddle surfing.

Lured from Pennsylvania to Waikiki for its warmth and a military job at Pearl Harbor in 1940, John Zapotocky became interested in stand up paddling after watching Duke and the AhChoys from the beach. John made himself at home in the warm waters of Hawaii and was active in swimming, diving, paddleboarding, and canoe racing. He became known as "Pearl Diver" for driving the front of his board into waves. He has kept his board on a rack on Waikiki Beach for more than sixty years. With the help of younger surfers who carry his board to the water, John still surfs his stand up board. Duke, John, and the AhChoys are known as the original "Beachboys" of Waikiki.

Despite the post-Gidget boom of the 1960s and then again in the 1980s, stand up paddling never stuck with surfers. It took modern pioneers such as Fletcher Burton and Dave Kalama to integrate the lessons of history with modern technology and style.

CORRAN ADDISON

Paddling since the age of eight, South African Corran Addison has competed in the Olympics as a whitewater slalom kayaker, won several world freestyle kayaking titles, and held the world record for ten years for kayaking off a 101-foot waterfall. An innovative designer, he started several leading kayak companies such as Savage, Riot, and Dagarossi and designed the first planing-hulled whitewater kayak.

In 1992, he started Imagine Surfboards in Montreal. In 2007, he discovered stand up paddling and found the perfect blend for his many water-based interests. Many of his SUP designs are the first of their kind, including rotomolded river boards and a SUP with a hatch that can be paddled as a sit-on-top kayak.

A perpetual traveller, Corran has surfed on every continent except Antarctica. He's most often found dropping into the huge bombs on the North Shore of Hawaii, running waterfalls on a SUP, and surfing the river wave, Habit 67, in Montreal. Corran lives in Dana Point, CA. Find out more about Corran on his website: www.imaginesurfboards.com.

Fletcher Burton stand up surfing his wave ski in Hawaii

Radical surfer-turned-wave-ski-surfer Fletcher Burton paddled into waves back in the late 1990s seated on an 8-foot-long wave ski. Once on the wave he would jump to his feet and surf like advanced stand up paddle surfers do today. However, negative stigma attached to seated surfers meant that no surfer was likely to take note of his style and ability to ride different kinds of waves. Had Burton been taken seriously, stand up paddle surfing might be ten years ahead of where it is now.

Perhaps it was the bigger names in surfing that finally gave stand up paddling some legitimacy. One day in 1995, big wave surfer Dave Kalama grabbed a short OC-1 (outrigger) paddle to try with his board. With such a short paddle, Dave and friend Laird Hamilton found themselves bent over in order to use the short paddles. Laird came back the next day with longer paddles he had built specifically, and the two began to see the benefits of stand up paddling. Shortly thereafter, other Hawaiian surfers such as Brian Keaulana, Rick Thomas, and Archie Kalepa, found stand up paddling to be effective training while the surf was down. As the years went by, these surfers found themselves entering events such as the Moloka'i to O'ahu Paddleboard Race and the Makaha Big Board Surfing Classic. With its growing popularity at Makaha Beach, Brian Keaulana decided to add "Beachboy Surfing" to the world recognized "Buffalo Big Board Contest" in 2004. The response was overwhelming, with more than forty-nine participants entering the stand-up division, including many of Hawaii's elite watermen. A photo of Laird Hamilton was snatched up by the surfing media, and in a matter of months the first stand up paddle surfing boom had begun.

Despite stand up paddling's roots in South American fishing cultures and in various Middle Eastern and African countries—as well as the modern spin-offs used for lifeguard rescue and other practical purposes—the modern version of Beach Boy paddle surfing remained a Hawaiian phenomenon until Vietnam veteran Rick Thomas brought a paddleboard back to California in 2000. It caught on instantly. Bob Long, from Mission Surf, has suggested that there are six degrees of separation between any California stand up paddler and Rick Thomas.

Stand up paddling has been a much needed breath of fresh air into an industry stuck in its 1960s glory days. Stolid, stale, and elitist, surfing had become a highly commercialized multimillion dollar machine. Everyone from Kansas to California was wearing surfing clothing and using surf lingo, while out on the waves newbies were not welcome in the surf lineup. To this day anyone not born within a 5-mile radius of any given break is shunned by "locals." Beginners are branded as "kooks" and are often driven from the beaches.

Stand up paddle surfing had instant appeal to all kinds of surfers. It allowed one to paddle to far away, little-known breaks, thus increasing the number of waves each surfer could have and the range of conditions that could be surfed. In fact, very quickly stand up paddlers realized that the "surf" could be taken out of it, and recreational and racing stand up paddling became sports unto themselves. All across the USA, Europe, and Australia, landlocked people started using SUPs as replacements for canoes or kayaks. By 2009 stand up paddleboarding was the fastest growing paddle sport in North America.

As a true indication that stand up paddling has "arrived," as of October 3, 2008, the US Coast Guard has classified SUPs as vessels, like canoes or kayaks. As a result, SUP riders are required to wear a personal flotation device (PFD) when paddling in certain areas outside of the surf zone.

CHAPTER 1

SUP boards on shore

GET YOUR GEAR ON

Like most sports, stand up paddling requires a fair amount of gear. As you begin your search for equipment that will meet your specific needs, you'll be met by a dizzying array of options. It's worth taking some time to figure out which gear is the best for you, because the right equipment will translate to more fun on the water.

STAND UP PADDLEBOARDS

The majority of stand up paddleboards (SUPs) are made from fiberglass and epoxy wrapped over a foam core. Inflatable, wood, plastic, and hollow fiberglass boards are also available. The boards have fins, like traditional surfboards, and a leash so the paddler won't lose the board in the water. The front of the board is called the nose, the rear is called the tail, the top is the deck, and the sides are referred to as the rails. The bottom is either the hull, or just the bottom.

BOTTOM OR HULL

The bottom shape of a stand up board helps determine stability and glide. Like surfboards, many SUPs come with a flat planing bottom. A V-bottom feels less stable but helps the board turn easier, and is ultimately more stable in rough water. This is called secondary stability. Some boards have V in the tail or only in the middle but flatten out to a planing hull. Some boards are now being built with a round-bottomed displacement hull similar to some kayaks or the very fast surf skis and paddleboards. Displacement hulls are faster than planing hulls because there's less surface area in the water, but they can be tippy if they are built narrow for racing.

NOSE

The nose is either pointy or round on stand up paddleboards. Round noses provide more surface area, thus more stability, but are often slower because the wider width pushes more surface area through the water in order to move forward. Pointy noses are often found on racing or touring boards with a displacement hull. The combination of the pointy nose and displacement hull creates what's called a knife-edged bow, or plum bow, which cuts through rather than over waves, or a sweeping bow, which extends over the water and floats over or above waves or choppy water. Pointy noses can also be found on boards called guns, allowing greater speed and less wind resistance when dropping in on fast, big waves.

RAILS

Rails are the sides of the board. Rails help determine stability in a variety of water. A downturned rail comes to an edge at the bottom of the board and will feel tippy, but will help turn the board more easily while moving or in surf. A round, rolled, or egg rail will be stable and forgiving, but slower to turn in moving water.

TAILS

There are four basic tails on stand up boards. The pin, often seen in racing boards, comes to a point in the center. A deep swallow, also referred to as a split pin, is used in "fish" surfboards. The swallow has a fish-tail shape, which makes it easier to turn than the pin and gives it lift and stability. It is most often used in surf to make fast, quick turns. Square tail boards are easy to turn and offer the most surface area. They are best in head-high surf and are the most common tail on SUPs. Another tail shape is the wing, which is actually on the rail. The wing reduces surface area in

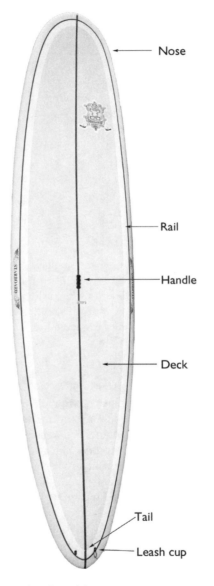

Stand up board features

the tail, making it easier to turn. Wings resemble a jagged edge cut in the rail 1–2 feet from the tail. Other types of tails include the diamond, rounded squashtail, and baby swallowtail.

DESIGN FEATURES

Stand up paddleboards are usually 4–5 inches thick. Thickness determines how much flotation the board has. A board that is too thick will be unstable due to a higher center of gravity; too thin and it will sink under your weight. Some boards have carved out decks that lower your center of gravity. These are common on race boards.

Rocker is the amount of curve from tail to nose, as seen from the side. The more rocker a board has the more easily it will turn, but it will be slower in flatwater. In flatwater, a higher nose will glide more easily over rough water. Less tail rocker helps the board track straighter, while more rocker in the tail helps it turn easier.

Foil is the change in thickness from the nose to the tail of the board. Many surf specific boards are now being made thicker in the tail to provide more flotation for turning the board on a wave. Most touring boards have the same thickness from nose to tail for greater stability.

Many boards are built with a combination of the above characteristics in order to achieve a specific function. For example, a board might have a pointy nose with a displacement hull in the front portion of the board, a planing bottom under the middle, a V in the tail, egg rails, and a deep swallow tail. There are dozens of surfboard shapers

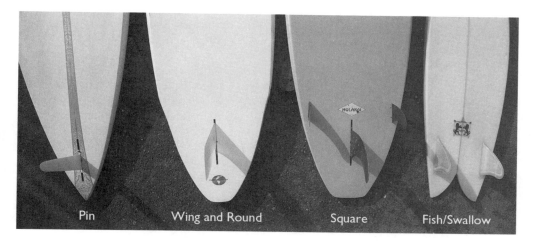

Pin | Wing and Round | Square | Fish/Swallow

The four basic tail shapes: pin, round, square, and swallow

regularly creating new and innovative designs.

Stand up paddleboards are available in a variety of sizes and designs. You must consider your height and weight, your skill level, and the type of water in which you plan to paddle in order to select the right one for you. But SUPs are also quite versatile, so it's possible to own one board for use in a variety of conditions, from flatwater to surf to rivers.

Stand up paddleboards are thicker and wider than traditional surfboards, allowing you to stand on the board without sinking it. The most common boards are between 10–12 feet long, 4–5 inches thick, and about 31 inches wide.

Boards made specifically for river use tend to be shorter to allow for quick turns through rapids and boulders. River boards are often rotomolded plastic or hard shell inflatables to protect the rails (sides) against rocks. Racing boards are narrower and range from 12-feet, 6-inches to 18-feet in length, and they are most often made from carbon fiber. There are also 6- to 10-foot boards that allow for more flexibility in the surf. Due to their shorter length, these boards tend to be very wide and thick. Boards for fishing are very wide and stable. There are even a few boards that allow for a mast attachment and tiller for sailing or wind surfing.

During the initial years when the sport began gaining public interest, boards resembled large surfboards with a planing or flat bottom. Recently, board designers have begun to design SUPs with displacement hulls (round bottom) and a pointed, raised nose similar to kayaks for greater stability, more speed, and for cutting through rough water. The sport has grown so fast in recent

Installing a fin in a board

years that new board designs are coming out monthly.

FINS

Fins are attached under the tail and sometimes in the middle of the board to help the board track straight. Fins also add control and balance to a board.

The fin setup you use depends on the type of water you're paddling. Many SUPs have a single fin, which is often best for flatwater or small surf. The longer the fin, the better the board tracks. Surfers use different fin arrangements depending on the type of waves they're surfing or the type of response they want from the board. Some river boards have rubber or retractable fins, to avoid breakage or entrapment between rocks. Some flatwater boards are being made with fins closer to the middle where the paddler stands; this displaces most of the paddler's weight for better control. Manufacturers are now making fins specifically for racing as well as kelp fins that are designed to avoid getting caught in kelp or weeds in a lake.

Some touring boards use skegs that can be drawn up inside the board and used at different lengths depending on the type of water or wind. A few race and downwinder boards have fins that can be controlled directionally by your feet from the deck of the board, like a rudder.

It is important to avoid paddling in water shallow enough to chip or break the fin. Also, when a fin drags on the bottom or gets caught in kelp or weeds, the board will stop and throw the paddler forward. When paddling in kelp or lake milfoil with a non-bungee leash, pull the extra slack in the leash up on the board and stand on it until you're clear of the obstruction.

SHAPER

A shaper is a person who designs and builds surfboards. A shaper uses sanding tools to shape a foam block to exact specifications. The shaper will cover the board in fiberglass and epoxy, then sand the board to create the finished board. To increase productivity, many shapers are now using 3D computer design programs and a CNC cutting machine, which can carve a foam block to precise specifications.

PADDLES

The paddle used with the SUP resembles a very long canoe paddle and should be 8–15 inches taller than the paddler. The paddle consists of a handle, shaft blade, and the power face. Paddles are made from a variety of materials, such as carbon fiber, fiberglass, and wood. The paddle shaft is often bent forward just above the blade to provide more forward reach into the water. Some paddle shafts are bent forward in the middle of the shaft as well as the blade to add even more reach, thus extra power to the stroke. Paddle shafts designed for stand up paddling are unique in that they have a stronger build to withstand the longer distance and extra tension from the lower hand to the water. In a decade of kayaking extremely rough water and surf, I've never broken a paddle, but I did break a kayak paddle shaft recently when testing it for stand up paddling on flatwater. Use SUP-specific paddles to avoid being stranded with a broken paddle.

The paddle blade is dihedral in shape, which makes it more efficient in the water. One-, two-, and three-piece paddles are available for easier storage. Paddle shafts can also be telescoping to allow adjustment.

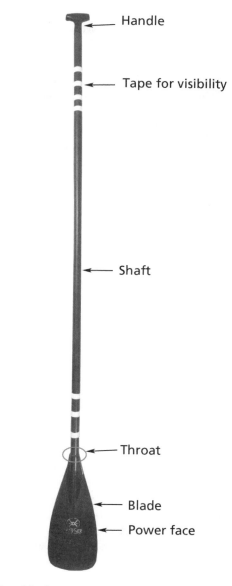

SUP paddle features

Handle

Tape for visibility

Shaft

Throat

Blade

Power face

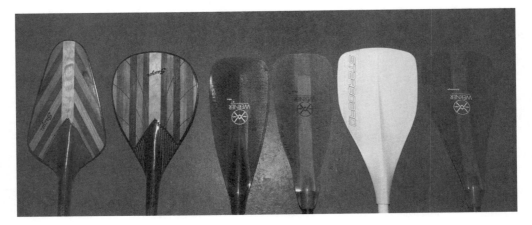

A selection of different types of SUP paddle blades

Some paddlers prefer a shorter paddle for surfing, or a longer paddle for racing or long-distance trips. Paddle blades vary in shape and width. Narrow-bladed paddles, often used for racing, produce less strain on your shoulders due to less resistance in the water. A shorter, faster cadence is required with a narrow-bladed paddle to make up for its lack of width. One of these paddles, the Ottertail, made by Werner's surfboard shaper Steve Boehne, has a pointed blade tip that allows variation in the depth of the paddle.

A few paddles have removable handles to allow you to add another blade to create a kayak paddle, in case you want to paddle sitting down. Paddle covers are available to prevent the edges of the blade from damaging the board. Some paddlers apply tape to the blade as an alternative. Carry an extra breakdown paddle on long trips in case your main paddle is broken or lost.

After purchasing a paddle, apply silver reflective tape on both sides of the blade to make yourself more visible to boaters both day and night. Some paddlers apply colorful tape to the paddle shaft in case it is lost in rough water. Bright colors such as yellow work well in whitewater.

LEASHES

It's important to use a leash with a SUP, as with a traditional surfboard. It prevents losing the board after a fall. Wind, surf, and river current can move an unleashed board away very quickly, thus endangering others in the surf zone or creating a possible rescue situation in open water. I once borrowed a friend's new board that had no leash, and after a fall the board took off downwind and out of reach. Luckily my friend was able to retrieve it.

Leashes should be the same length as or slightly shorter than the board. One end of the leash wraps around your ankle or thigh with a Velcro strap, and the other end connects to the tail of the board. Bungee leashes are used to prevent the leash from dragging in the water. River paddlers might consider avoiding leashes because they are prone to snagging on boulders or logs and creating potentially lethal traps. Leashes can break, particularly in large surf where wipeouts are common.

If you're landing or launching your board in rough water, hold on to the board end of the leash to prevent losing the board prior to climbing on. This is called short leashing.

PERSONAL FLOTATION DEVICES (PFDS)

In 2008, the U.S. Coast Guard determined that stand up paddlers outside of surf zones are required to wear lifejackets, also called Personal Flotation Devices (PFDs). You should use a Coast Guard approved Type 2 or 3 PFD, which are available at most surf, boating, and kayak shops.

PFDs provide not only flotation but also insulation in colder temperatures, and collision protection in the surf zone. In the case of a dislocated shoulder, severe hypothermia, or loss of consciousness, a PFD will also keep your head above water until help arrives.

Some stand up paddlers resist wearing PFDs and attach them to their boards in order

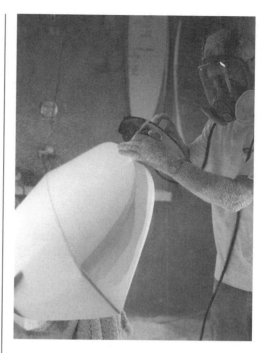

Steve Boehne of Infinity Surfboards, shaping a SUP

to pass inspection by the Coast Guard or their local water police. However, in a true emergency, these paddlers will be ill-equipped and may not have enough time to untie their PFDs from the boards, particularly in rough or cold water. If you do tie your PFD to your board, use a quick-release system instead of duct tape or rope to allow for speedy removal of the PFD in case of emergency. Check the regulations in your area.

Some paddlers claim that PFDs are uncomfortable, while others find them too hot. However, there are many models available, and it's worth doing some research to find a PFD that works for you. Whitewater kayakers need a lot of shoulder flexibility, so PFDs made for that sport are minimalist and allow for full arm and shoulder movement.

Some paddlers argue that the SUP itself is a flotation device, and that as long as a leash is used there is little chance of losing the board.

For those who prefer a minimalist PFD, check out the waist belts that resemble a small fanny pack. These are Type 2 PFDs, the only PFDs that will keep your head above the surface if you're unconscious. Pulling the handle that dangles outside the pouch will trigger a C02 cartridge and inflate the PFD. These resemble the Mae West lifejackets seen on airplanes. The downside is that they lack thermal protection. They should be rinsed after use in saltwater to prevent corrosion of the pull-tab mechanism.

Kayaking lifejackets, which are Type 3 PFDs, are the most versatile on the market and come with multiple pockets that allow you to store safety items such as energy bars, flares, a whistle, or even a VHF radio. Rescue PFDs, often found at kayak shops, are equipped to allow a towline bag with a quick-release strap that attaches around the waist. Kayaking PFDs also have attachment points on the exterior to attach lights, knives, or other items. I attach a mini waterproof LED light on my rear shoulder for night paddling. Boating shops sell another inflatable Type 2 PFD that either inflates automatically when you fall in the water, or can be inflated using a hand triggered C02 device. These PFDs have two long sections of fabric that fit vertically over your chest, and are common with sailors and flat-water surf ski racers. Kitesurfers and wakeboarders often use pocketless Coast Guard-approved PFDs such as the O'Neill Assault Vest, which has full coverage over the chest. The term "impact vest" is used for essentially any PFD with a foam core that protects your body from a fall on rocks, a reef, or in large waves.

Select a colorful PFD with silver reflector strips for better visibility. Vest PFDs should fit snugly around your chest, but not so tightly that breathing is affected. Adjust the straps so the PFD doesn't slide up to your chin or over your head while in the water. If paddling in saltwater, wash your PFD with freshwater regularly to protect the fabric, zipper, and plastic buckles from corrosion.

STUFF TO CARRY IN YOUR PFD

PFDs are usually blessed with a multitude of pockets, which allow the intrepid paddler to amply prepare for almost any conditions. What follows is a list of important items to consider carrying in your PFD. While some items may not fit in pockets, they can be attached to the PFD using string or a carabiner.

Waterproof, floating VHF (Very High Frequency) radio. Find one that will fit in your PFD pocket. Many VHFs aren't actually waterproof, so store it in a waterproof bag just in case. VHF radios are used to contact the Coast Guard, to check the weather, and to monitor shipping traffic when crossing busy waterways. Check your batteries regularly and rinse with freshwater to prevent saltwater corrosion. Learn how to use the VHF so you can act quickly in an emergency. Every coastal and inland waterway has a specific channel that monitors local shipping traffic. You can call the Coast Guard to ask for shipping info and to state your position and destination so other vessels will know of your presence, especially in fog or at night. Channel 16 is reserved for emergencies. The Coast Guard will announce storm warnings on channel 16, then channel 22a. If in imminent danger, use channel 16 and say "Mayday" three times, list your location, describe your type of craft, the problem, and end with "over." Repeat every two minutes. Other important call words are "Pan Pan," for a difficult situation with possible injury; and "Securite Securite," for a dangerous situation between ships or marine craft.

In 2006, a friend and I rescued a boater who had flipped his fishing boat in the frigid waters of Puget Sound. He was nearly blue when we found him. I called Mayday on channel 16, described the situation to the Coast Guard, our location, etc., and within a few minutes a police boat was headed our way. I shot an aerial flare to mark our location.

Handheld rocket aerial flares. Flares are used to signal for help. It's common for a flare not to fire, so have at least three on hand. Store them in a waterproof bag or two ziplock bags. Replace your flares at least once a year as water or condensation can ruin them. In case of emergency, shoot one to get attention, then another to help rescuers find you. Handheld traffic flares drip sparks that can ruin your board or burn you. Flares shot by a gun are difficult to stow on a board. Learn how to use your flares prior to setting out.

Whistle. Attach a whistle to the exterior of your PFD. Don't rely on the whistle alone, because in high wind it may be difficult to hear. Buy a whistle without the pea inside.

Cell Phone. Cell phones are a great complement to the VHF. If you live in non-coastal areas, a cell phone will be your only way to contact others in an emergency. I use a small plastic peanut butter jar with a screw top to store my phone. It's waterproof and floats.

Energy bars. I usually have at least one in my PFD in case I get hungry. In extreme cold, food helps to keep you warm.

Waterproof LED light. Keep one attached to the exterior of your PFD for night paddling. Attaching it behind your shoulder will prevent it from affecting your night vision. A single white light is required for night paddling in many areas. I also keep a waterproof flashlight in my front pocket to shine at boaters or for assistance in night navigation. Larger lights can be attached to your board with a suction cup. Attach a safety line to your leash cup in case the suction cup fails. Blinking lights are illegal in most areas; check your local regulations on night paddling. Bicycling lights are an option; they are bright and often waterproof.

Hiker's compass. Helpful for navigation or when disoriented in fog.

Polarized sunglasses. I use cheap sunglasses as I tend to lose or step on them. Attach a floating retainer strap in case they fall in the water.

Neoprene skull cap or hood. In case of immersion, rain, or cold weather. There are several warm neoprene hoods and half hoods with chin straps available at surfing and kayaking shops.

A properly fitted PFD

Sun block and lip balm. Use products with at least a 30 SPF. Zinc oxide is best for complete protection.

Metal signal mirror. Can be used to reflect sunlight to signal for help, or to warn an oncoming powerboat.

Compact emergency mylar blanket. These products provide wind protection and can be a great visual aid to attract attention. Large, thick, plastic survival bags and compact sleeping bags are also available.

Chemical heat packs or hand warmers. Place in a ziplock bag to prevent corrosion.

Waterproof watch. Attach to the exterior of your PFD to help track tidal changes.

Tide table and navigational chart. Store in a waterproof bag or ziplock bag.

Chemical light stick. Can be used for night paddling or to signal for help. Tie the stick to a string and swing in a circle to attract attention.

Multi-tool. Can be carried in place of knife that would be used to cut fishing lines, nets, etc., and includes a screwdriver to use in attaching or tightening the screws on the fin.

Waterproof camera. There are many to choose from. Bright colors are helpful for locating the camera, and having one small enough to fit in a PFD pocket is nice, too.

Hydration pack. Great for staying hydrated. Consider adding an electrolyte tablet to prevent muscle cramping.

Small roll of duct tape. For board, paddle, or PFD repairs. Who doesn't love duct tape? Flatten the roll to be more compact.

Stainless steel carabiner. Some paddlers attach these to the PFD shoulder strap to assist in rescues on the river or open water.

Waterproof emergency strobe light. Attach to your rear shoulder. These are for emergencies only, as flashing lights are illegal in many areas.

Waterproof laser pointer. Used to shine into pilot houses of boats that don't see you. Use only for emergencies, as the laser can damage a person's eyes. The batteries burn out quickly.

Ear plugs. Many surfers get "surfer's ear," which requires surgery to fix. Silicone ear plugs are probably the best for keeping water out and are cheap, but they cut your hearing by at least 90 percent. Plastic ear plugs have tiny holes that help with hearing while reducing water seepage into your ear.

Attach every item to a string to prevent loss during immersion. The string should be long enough to properly use the item but not long enough to go around your neck.

GEAR STORAGE: PACKS AND BAGS

Even for short paddles in your local waters, it's nice to bring along not only the essentials but also a few luxuries, such as a picnic lunch or a larger camera. I've listed below a variety of options available for carrying whatever you need while you're on the water.

Some contents of a PFD: knife, light, whistle, flares, compass, hood, chemical hand warmer, duct tape, signaling mirror, emergency blanket, carabiner, and energy bar.

FANNY PACKS

Fanny packs are useful for carrying essential items such as bottled water, a waterproof camera, and extra supplies. If you choose to not use a PFD, consider carrying the items listed in the PFD section in the fanny pack. Make sure the pack drains water and doesn't

Some contents for a fanny pack: emergency flares, compass, duct tape, carabiner, hood, knife, chemical hand warmers, emergency blanket, signaling mirror, and energy bar

BACKPACKS

Many sport shops carry minimalist backpacks designed for activities such as trail running or climbing. Water bottles can be attached to the packs, and many have hydration bladders. Unlike a fanny pack, these backpacks distribute the weight more evenly on your back and carry a bit more gear. Some models are waterproof. Since many of these packs weren't designed for paddling, consider cutting small holes in the bottom to allow for drainage, and add a waterproof light on the exterior for night paddling. Some packs have waterproof zippers or a roll top like a dry bag.

DECK BAGS

Deck bags are great for carrying extra gear on the deck of your board, rather than on your back or waist. There are several models available, including waterproof options to keep your things dry. Deck bags are sealed by either a waterproof zipper or a roll and snap enclosure. Keep important items such as a VHF radio or your cell phone in a separate waterproof bag. Deck bags are often found in kayaking stores.

slide up to the chest during a swim. You can purchase a runner's fanny pack and cut small holes in the pockets to allow water to drain. Silver reflector tape is recommended for visibility. For night paddling, attach a waterproof light to the exterior of the pack. Some fanny packs have built in hydration bladders. You can also attach the fanny pack to your board.

DRY BAGS

Dry bags are waterproof fabric bags that close by rolling the opening and snapping the ends together with a buckle. They have fewer attachment points but are still useful and more affordable than a deck bag for carrying extra clothing or other items.

Properly equipped, paddlers enjoy hours of surfing on their stand up paddleboards.

CLOTHING

Your clothing will vary depending on water temperature and weather conditions. If you're surfing in warm water you may not need a wet suit to be comfortable, but if you're surfing in frigid temperatures you'll need to dress carefully to prevent hypothermia. Stand up paddling can be a workout, and many people find that they need less thermal protection than they expect. But it's a good idea to carry extra clothing just in case.

Consider adding tie downs to your board (see chapter 3, Flatwater Paddling) for carrying extra clothing in a dry bag, or carry extra clothing in a fanny pack. In colder climates avoid cotton, which provides no warmth when wet. Synthetic materials such as fleece, neoprene, Polartec, capilene, and polypropylene will keep you warm when wet. Wool will also keep you warm, but it's heavy and smelly when wet. There are a few wool products now that offer a thin insulating layer that resembles the synthetic products. When it comes to dry or wet suits, try before you buy. Rent a few options to see which works best for you.

WARM WATER

Warm water paddling requires less gear, but you still need to take precautions. Wear a light- or white-colored UV-protection rash guard to protect your skin from the sun and keep you cooler. Since rash guards are tight, they will not flap in the wind and will adhere to the skin should you take an unplanned swim.

A wide-brimmed, light-colored hat is recommended to keep the sun out of your eyes and to keep your head cooler. A waterproof, 30 SPF or higher shirt, hat, or pants will also help. Polarized sunglasses with a floating retainer are recommended, and consider floating sunglasses if available. If you need prescription sunglasses, waterproof sunglasses are available that wrap around the head like goggles.

Neoprene paddling booties or reef walkers protect your feet from hot sand and sharp coral. They also add grip to the board.

Some paddlers wear a neoprene top and shorts, or a shorty 2–3 mm wet suit that has minimal arm and leg protection.

Warning: Heat stroke is a form of hyperthermia that can lead to death. Hyperthermia is caused by the body producing more heat than it can dissipate. Symptoms include dizziness, nausea, fatigue, and delirium. Seek immediate medical attention if this occurs. Prevention includes drinking plenty of water or sports drinks with electrolytes prior to, during, and after exercise. Hydration tablets in water are also helpful. Light-colored cotton clothing and a hat can help as well. You might want to avoid exercise altogether in severely hot weather.

COLD WATER

In places like the Pacific Northwest, where I live, weather can change very quickly from calm to gale-force winds, causing a drop in air temperature and an increase in wave size. Year-round water temperatures range from 45 to 60 degrees F, and three

STEVE BOEHNE

In 1964 while living in Virginia for his senior year in high school, California native Steve Boehne decided to stand on his 12-foot tandem board using a long canoe paddle to get around on local lakes. He wore full winter clothes in winter to stay warm. Steve had learned to surf in 1959 in Torrance Beach and Palos Verdes Cove, and his first board was a balsa Velzy-Jacobs. Steve learned to shape boards with the help of a sixteen-year-old neighbor and his father, who were making garage boards. By 1967 Steve had built nearly one hundred boards in his garage, and he landed his first shaping job for Gordie Surfboards in Huntington Beach in 1968. A master craftsman, Gordie taught Steve how to build the classic longboard shapes.

(Photo courtesy Infinity Surfboards)

In the late 1960s, Steve and his new wife Barrie opened their first Infinity Surfboards shop in an old gas station along the Pacific Coast Highway in Huntington Beach. Now based in nearby Dana Point, Infinity has handcrafted more than thirty thousand boards. Steve's sons Dan and Dave are an intregal part of the business and are often seen on their blog dropping into waves near their shop and across the globe.

Infinity began building stand up paddleboards in 2005. With the help of a CNC machine, which reduces much of the repetitive labor required in building boards, they are able to keep up with all the SUP orders, making nearly two thousand boards a year. They've also co-designed a surfing paddle with Werner Paddles called the Ottertail, which reduces shoulder stress and allows for a higher cadence. Their SUPs include a high-performance super-light carbon racing board, a tandem board, shorter surfing SUPs, and an all-around board for flatwater or surfing. Infinity also makes surfboards and wave skis. In 2010 they made a board with steerable tiller on the nose.

When asked how to choose your first SUP, Steve suggests determining what type of padding you want to do. For surfing only, get a board 11 feet or shorter. For flatwater paddling get a board longer than 11 feet. For both surfing and flatwater, get an 11-foot board. He also suggests that the most important surf stroke to learn is the pivot "wheely" turn, which allows you to turn the board around quickly when you see the wave you want to catch. For more information, go to www.infinitysurf.com.

Patrick Aio is dressed for chilly conditions.

tidal cycles flush the Puget Sound each day, making it frigid even on the hottest days of summer. Only the lakes warm up to comfortable swimming temperatures in late summer.

In conditions like these, if you fall in the water without a wet suit or a dry suit, you can lose feeling in your hands in minutes. You'll begin to feel the effects of hypothermia in twenty minutes.

It is important to dress for immersion and carry extra clothing. Some people stay warmer than others, so you should follow your own instincts about what to wear. Over the years, I've had a few situations where I asked my friends what they were wearing, did the same, and nearly froze. I've also had other paddlers ask me why I'm not wearing more clothes on hot summer days with water temps in the seventies. I tend to get colder than others, so I always carry an extra neoprene hood and Gore-Tex dry top. I'd rather be too warm than too cold. If I get hot, I can always jump in and cool off.

Warning: Hypothermia is a condition in which your body temperature drops below what is required for normal metabolism and bodily function. Signs of hypothermia include severe shivering, slurred speech, blue lips, loss of control, and slowed breathing. Inadequate attention can lead to death. Drowning occurs when you lose control of your hands and limbs, and thus can't swim. Prevention includes dressing appropriately, wearing a fleece hat or neoprene hood, bringing hot drinks or soup in a thermos, wearing a PFD, and carrying extra clothing for emergencies.

DRY SUITS

Dry suits are one-piece suits made from Gore-Tex and other breathable fabrics. They have waterproof latex or neoprene gaskets at the wrists, ankles, and neck to keep a paddler mostly dry. Synthetic clothing such as fleece and capilene are worn underneath for insulation. Gore-Tex dry suits can also be dried in the sun very quickly. Some dry suits also come with a waterproof pee zipper. Additional options include Gore-Tex booties that are attached to the suit or a hood.

Dry suits aren't always completely dry, though, as you can get wet from perspiration and from tiny leaks in worn gaskets or fabric. They also require maintenance to keep the latex gaskets in good condition. The waterproof zippers and Gore-Tex also require maintenance. Dry suits vary in quality, and cost from $400 to $1,200. Choose a bright-colored dry suit with silver reflector strips to make you more visible on the water.

While dry suits with a zippered rear drop seat are made for women, some women use a feminine urinal directional device (FUD) which allows them to use a men's suit as well.

Before putting your dry suit on, spray the inside and outside of the gaskets with a lubricant such as 303 Aerospace Lubricant to allow an easier fit over your head. Once your head is through the narrow opening, carefully pull the neck gasket away from your neck and squat to your knees to "burp" the extra air out. An air-filled suit can make for uncomfortable paddling. If your suit keeps filling with air, you might have a leak in the fabric or gaskets. You can repair such leaks with Gore-Tex fabric tape or products such as Aquaseal. You can also send the dry suit to the manufacturer for repair. Wash the suit weekly inside and out with freshwater to prevent corrosion of the fabric, zippers, and gaskets.

WET SUITS

Full-size surfing wet suits have come a long way in recent years, with super stretchy Japanese limestone neoprene and surprisingly warm insulation, including some lined with Merino wool that match and in some cases surpass the warmth of a dry suit. I use a wet suit as I prefer the low maintenance and stretchy material that works great for kayaking as well as stand up paddling. Wet suits are priced much lower than dry suits; they range from $250 to $600. Some have various accessories, such as attached hoods. The only regular maintenance needed for wet suits is rinsing in freshwater after each use.

Wet suit warmth is measured by the thickness of the neoprene. A suit 2- to 3-mm thick is good for slightly chilly water while you might want a thicker suit for water in the 35- to 50-degree range. Some wet suits have varying thickness: a 5/4, for example, is 5-mm thick in the chest while the arms and legs are 4 mm. A 5/4/3 has a 5-mm chest, 4-mm leg, and 3-mm arm. Many of today's suits are thinner but much warmer than older, thicker suits. With some products, a 3 mm is now as warm as a 5/4 from a few years ago. Each person's body reacts to cold differently, so rent and try different thicknesses before purchasing.

Many paddlers think wet suits are not flexible in terms of adding warmth. Wet suit warmth can be increased by wearing capilene or a thin crewneck fleece shirt underneath. Adding a kayaking style Gore-Tex paddling jacket will increase your core temperature by 10 to 20 degrees. I wear a 4/3 mm suit with a capilene top underneath and a neoprene hooded vest for winter in the Puget Sound region. In extreme wind chill, I'll add a Gore-Tex paddling jacket that I keep on my deck in a dry bag under bungees. If I don't need it, usually a friend will after realizing he has dressed too lightly for the conditions.

There are also a few battery-powered warmed wet suits and accessories that have been given rave reviews for their warmth.

COMBO WET SUIT AND DRY TOP

For years paddlers have worn an effective combination of a sleeveless 3-mm wet suit, called a Farmer John/Jane, and a Gore-Tex paddling jacket. Neoprene or fleece shirts are worn underneath the suit for additional warmth. Remove or add a layer of clothing depending on weather conditions. This combination is the most affordable of the above clothing options, but not the warmest if you are immersed in cold water for long periods of time. Look for paddling jackets that don't have the inner tube fabric layer, which are meant to attach to spray skirts on kayaks. This option costs from $200 to $300. Another alternative is to wear

HOW TO PUT ON A WET SUIT

Most people who try a wet suit for the first time put it on backwards. I once did a photo shoot of three model surfers who had their wet suits on backwards. None of us knew until the client in Los Angeles noticed it when she reviewed the photos. Today's wet suits are flexible and affordable, making them an ideal garment to keep for cold water sports.

There are two types of wet suits. The most common suit and easiest to get into has a zipper on the upper back that is closed using a long string that you pull up behind you. If you can't reach the zipper string, have a friend close it, or find a way to wrap the string around a door knob, then squat on the floor to close the zipper. Some paddlers think zippers leak and wear down over time. Some wet suits are also made without zippers. They are tougher to get into, but are drier and warmer.

The best way to get into a wet suit is to fold back the open shoulder areas like peeling a banana. Step one leg into the suit and pull the ankle opening of the suit up around your lower leg. Then step your other leg in the other side. Standing, pull the suit up to your waist, smoothing out any wrinkles or folds in the neoprene. Put one arm in, then the other. For your booties, roll up the lower leg section of the suit to your shin, pull on your booties, then roll the neoprene of the suit down on top of your booties. Overlapping like this will help keep water out.

To remove the suit, unzip it first and, without stretching the neck collar too much, gently wrap the neoprene down from your neck and shoulders to your waist. Then roll the rest of the suit to your ankles.

Wash your suit with freshwater after every use. If you pee in your suit, wash it immediately after paddling with dish soap or wet suit soap. Otherwise your suit will smell funky for the rest of its life. Drip dry your suit after use. Machine drying it or blow drying may melt the material. If your suit isn't dry by the next time you use it, take a hot shower before getting into it.

a water-resistant rain shell over a Farmer John/Jane. While this is a more affordable option than a paddling jacket, it provides less protection from cold water.

PADDLING PANTS

Paddling pants are often made from Gore-Tex and other waterproof fabrics. They have a neoprene waistline and Velcro straps or neoprene at the ankles to keep water out. Many paddlers wear a dry top with the pants for full protection. In cold weather or long trips, I pack paddling pants in a dry bag as a backup. They're also useful in camp when it's raining.

FOOTWEAR

Beaches can be rocky or covered in sharp barnacles, and urban beaches are littered with broken glass, pieces of metal, and other foreign materials. In these environments it's wise to have thick neoprene booties with a sturdy outer sole to protect your feet. Some booties have additional ankle support and thick insulation for frigid water. In addition to what you find at your local surf shop, many kayak retailers have great options. Surfers often wear split-toed booties to allow for more control on the board. Chota makes an almost knee-high neoprene bootie that protects your lower leg and has a sturdy sole to prevent slippage on rocks or seaweed. Place cedar sachets in the booties when you store them to keep the stink out.

In warm temperatures many paddlers go barefoot or wear sandals to protect their feet from hot sand or rough pavement. In coral reef environments, a rubber soled shoe or bootie is highly recommended.

GLOVES

Neoprene gloves are a necessity for cold weather paddling. Gloves come in various thicknesses, can be fleece lined, and may have Velcro wrist straps to prevent slippage. Some paddlers use fingerless gloves for improved dexterity. I've even seen a few paddlers using rubber kitchen gloves, which have great grip and keep your hands dry.

HOODS AND SKULL CAPS

Hoods and skull caps add essential warmth to the head and neck areas, and are important if you are surfing or paddling in cold climates, or are new to the sport and more likely to fall in cold water. I carry a neoprene hood in my PFD that takes up little room but is there if I need it. I also use a skull cap with a sun visor, which is helpful on cold, bright days. Some wet suits come with attached hoods, and hooded neoprene vests are also available to wear over or under your suit.

Hoods also come in materials that are lighter and more windproof than traditional neoprene as well as in different colors, including high visibility orange that would be useful on busy waterways. Dive shops have the warmest hoods, but they might be too stiff if you're turning your head a lot to look for waves. Check kayak, dive, and surf shops for products available.

HATS

If you don't plan on jumping in and need only light protection from the elements, consider a water-resistant, wide-brimmed rain hat. Some have a fleece lining on the inside and also double as sun hats. Some people also wear ski hats or wool beanies. I also wear a baseball cap to keep the sun out of my eyes on milder days.

HELMETS

Helmets protect your head from injury in a fall onto rocks or coral, and from impact from your own paddle or board. SUPs are big and heavy, and even experienced paddlers fall regularly in surf and on rivers. Helmets also offer great wind-chill protection. I prefer a helmet with good ear protection.

RENTING EQUIPMENT

Rental boards tend to get a lot of abuse, and most rental shops use lower-quality boards. If you do rent, check the gear for

STAYING WARM

Rule number 1: make sure you're warm *before* you get on the water. Rule 2: maintain your core temperature as soon as you're off the water. Here are some suggestions for staying warm on land before and after you paddle.

BEFORE THE PADDLE:

1. Cut a foam camping pad in half and stand on it while putting your gear on. It really helps.
2. Leave your hat and coat on until you absolutely have to remove them.
3. Put your gloves on before unloading your board from the car.
4. Eat energy bars, trail mix, or drink a hot beverage before you paddle.

AFTER THE PADDLE:

1. Put your board on the car *first* and tie it down, then remove your wet suit, PFD, hood, etc.
2. Enjoy a thermos of warm soup or hot drink in the car. Avoid alcohol because it will make you colder.
3. Remove your wet suit while standing on your foam camping pad.
4. Rinse yourself off with a gallon of hot water.
5. Start your car as soon as you get off the water and turn the heater on. It'll be warm by the time you're ready to drive home.
6. Store some energy bars or other munchies in the car to refuel your body.
7. Keep dry clothes, fleece, and a down jacket in the car.
8. Have a backup key stored in a secret spot.
9. Keep a headlamp in the car to assist with tying the board on the car after dark. Keep extra batteries stored in the car.
10. Sounds a little strange, but stand by your running car's exhaust pipe to keep your legs warm. Don't burn yourself!
11. If you live nearby, leave your suit on to wash it off at home in the shower. Bring a towel to sit on in the car.

broken parts before taking it out of the store. Make sure paddle handles are secured to the shaft.

Also make sure the rental board comes with a leash that is as long as the board, and that the leash is securely attached. Check to make sure the leash's Velcro strap fits comfortably and securely around your ankle or thigh. Bring your own leash if you're not sure.

Contact the rental shop prior to going there to find out if they have wet suits, dry suits, or PFDs to use with the board, as well as water bottles, energy bars, sun block, lip balm, sunglasses retainers, or any other useful items that will help make your rental

Tail lift and carry technique

experience comfortable and safe. If they don't, bring your own. Many shops don't rent booties or hoods, or their gear is in poor shape. Check everything before you go. Wet suit booties and gloves tend to be one size smaller than listed on the product, so ask for a larger size. Bring your own capilene or wool socks as a filler or to keep your feet warmer in case there's a hole.

If the rental shop offers dry suits, remember that the latex gaskets can be tight and uncomfortable around your neck. Remove it immediately if you begin to feel lightheaded or dizzy. Some shops offer a round plastic tube to place in the gasket to make it wider. Only a small amount of water will get in if you go for a swim. Make sure your zippers work and are fully closed before getting on the water. Most rental wet suits and dry suits feel awkward, especially if you're not used to them.

Make sure you wash all your rental gear after use with freshwater, and dry by hanging over a clothesline or hanger.

PICKING UP AND CARRYING YOUR BOARD

SUPs are so wide and long that they may be difficult to carry under your arm. Many boards are quite heavy as well, but there are a few carrying techniques that will help. Some boards have loops to secure both ends of the paddle. Others also come with a hand grip in the middle of the board for easier carrying. There are a few shoulder strap products available that wrap around the board. Carrying a board in wind can be tricky, and it's best to limit your carrying distance if you're not in good physical shape. To protect your back, always make sure you bend your knees while lifting the board. Place your board deck-down if you have a traction pad, and deck-up if it's waxed.

Many boards come with a plastic carrying handle on the deck. Handles make carrying a board much easier, but there are some tips to be more efficient. While still in waist-deep water, flip the board on its side with the deck facing away from you. Reach your hand over the rail and grab the handle, then walk out of the water. This will prevent you from having to lean over and pick up the board, which will save your back in the long run. If your board doesn't come with carrying handles, there are several products available that allow you to attach fabric handles. If you know a reliable surfboard shaper, he should be able to attach a plastic handle to your board. In wind it's easier to carry your board on your head.

TAIL LIFT TECHNIQUE

Another method involves lifting the board from its tail and working your hands up the board until you can grab the rails in the middle with both hands. Place the top of your head in the middle of the board and lift to balance on your head. You can also use this method to lift the board onto your shoulder. To put the board down, put the nose of the board on the ground, then slowly walk your hands to the tail, setting the board gently down.

SHOULDER CARRY

With knees bent, bend over at the board's middle and tilt it on its side. With one hand, grab the rail from underneath while holding the top rail with your other hand. If you can't grab the bottom rail, rest the board on your feet, then lift to balance on your shoulder with your head tilted to one side. Carry the paddle in either hand. To put the board down, reverse the process.

There are several products available that allow for attaching a fabric strap over and under your board to allow for a shoulder carry. One product even comes with its own fanny pack.

Shoulder carrying technique

Paddle carrying technique

PADDLE CARRY

Some boards come with fabric loops to hold the paddle across the board. You can also attach the loops yourself, (see chapter 3, Flatwater Paddling). In this manner you may use the paddle as a handle.

TWO PERSON CARRY

If the above techniques don't work for you, ask for help carrying your board to the beach or to the car. With a person at each

end, lift the board by bending your knees. Don't lift the board using the leash, as it may damage the leash attachment loop, the leash cup, or fin box.

WHEELS

A few products have wheels that attach to one side of the board, allowing you to tow or pull the board on pavement. The Sticky Wheel has a suction cup that attaches to the board's bottom, while a strap secures it from the top. Some boards have a wheel built into the board. I've also seen paddlers on bicycles towing their boards strapped to baby carriages.

TRANSPORTING YOUR BOARD

Many bag options are available for carrying a board to your local paddling spot or for air travel. Most have shoulder carrying straps and are lined with foam to protect the board. For air travel, you might consider wrapping some bubble wrap around the board before putting it in the bag. Paddles can be placed in some bags, or carried separately in protected paddle bags. Check with your airline for any regulations or protocol for shipping boards.

Although they are longer and wider than a traditional surfboard, SUPs are carried in the same way on a car, strapped to the top either on a rack or directly on the roof. Make sure the deck faces down and the fin is up on the front side of your car. This helps the board from slipping out of the straps if tied too loosely. The most affordable way to strap on a board is to put a beach towel on the roof of the car, and extend two ropes or straps over the board and through the windows of the car. You can buy a padded strap

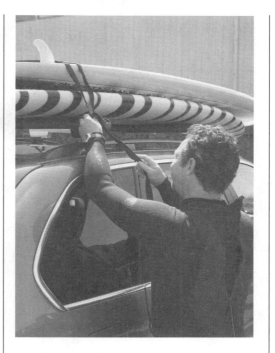

Tying boards to the roof rack

for the car roof, which buckles to secure the straps together through the windows in the car. Other paddlers use a fixed metal sport rack, padded with pipe insulation foam or various rack products. Kayak, surf, and sport rack shops have many rack options, as well as cable and lock products to secure your boards to the car.

CHAPTER 2

Youthful paddlers on Elliott Bay in Seattle, Washington

HOW TO STAND AND PADDLE: BASIC AND ADVANCED STROKES

Learning to stand up paddle is in some ways easier than a lot of other water sports, but as with any sport, some will pick it up more easily than others depending on athletic ability or experience in other water sports such as kayaking or surfing. Someone once told me you'll learn 70 percent of most stand up paddling skills in your first week of paddling; the rest depends on specific skills needed for surfing, rivers, rough water situations, racing, or long-distance paddling.

SURFERS LEARNING TO STAND UP PADDLE

If you're a surfer, you'll find that SUPs are big, heavy, and difficult to paddle while prone. Stand up paddling also requires more gear. Most surfers have never used a paddle and find that when surfing a SUP they use

the paddle to get out in the water, but forget to use it when surfing in. Learning efficient forward and turning strokes can take time. Surfers tend to approach stand up paddling on flatwater with their guard down, thinking it's easy, thus leaving the leash at home and dressing lighter than usual. Many refuse to wear PFDs. They often try to paddle too far on their first day, only to find that it's harder than expected. Stand up paddling outside of the surf zone is more like sea kayaking in that it requires knowledge of local tides, currents, and weather.

The advantage for surfers is that stand up paddling allows them to see further to spot waves sets, to catch waves much earlier, and to surf much smaller waves. A friend of mine says that stand up paddling gives him the opportunity to surf more often by allowing him to take advantage of local freighter or wind waves in a region where a drive to the coast is three hours away. SUPs also allow him access to surf breaks that would have required a boat before.

KAYAKERS LEARNING TO STAND UP PADDLE

For those with kayaking experience, stand up paddling shares common paddle strokes such as sweep turns, bow or stern rudders, and the dufek. Kayakers can also apply torso rotation for turns and the forward stroke, brace with the paddle, and edge their board to benefit turning. They will find that stand up paddling is a better core and leg workout. Stand up paddling is also great for improving balance, which is a benefit for kayaking as well.

The flip side is that kayakers' patience will be tested when dealing with an 11- or 12-foot board, which is much slower than a 17-foot sea kayak. Sea kayakers will have to work harder to paddle the distances they're used to, possibly even shorten their distances until they build their strength. Learning to surf will also be a challenge as SUP surfing is very similar to longboarding, which requires not only basic surf knowledge but also learning how to fall off the board, strong balance skills to be able to carve down wave faces, and good turning skills to avoid hazards such as other surfers.

STARTING OUT

Beginning paddlers should try the widest board possible in order to gain confidence and stability. A 30- to 36-inch-wide by 11- to 12-foot-long board is a good size to start with. Shorter paddlers can use a 10-foot board, which will be easier to manage.

Paddler's box; how to determine hand placement on the paddle

Some boards are very stable, while others might feel a little tippy until you gain your balance, which will come with water time. The first time I tried a board, in Hawaii, it was super tippy. I couldn't stand up, became discouraged, and didn't try again for a while. Later, near my home, I tried a wider, more stable board and stood up immediately.

It's best to learn and practice on flat-water before trying rough conditions. Starting out, you might fall often, so dress for the water temperature. In cold water make sure you're wearing a wet suit or dry suit. Also remember to wear your leash, as a fall, especially in wind, can push a board away from you very quickly. Always wear a PFD, and never go out in water conditions that are above your skill or comfort level. Avoid going out alone.

HOLDING THE PADDLE

Hold the paddle handle with one hand, and grab the shaft with the other. Your hands should be about 2 feet apart. Then place the paddle on the top of your head with your hands evenly spaced on each side. Your forearms should be vertical with your elbows bent at 90 degrees, creating what's called the paddler's box.

While paddling, keep the angled blade face facing away from you. Keep a loose grip with both hands, which not only prevents tendonitis but will also focus your energy elsewhere. Paddling is more about finesse than pure power. Rotating your torso slightly will provide power as you stroke.

To prevent tension in your wrists, don't let your hand sag below the handle. Keep the plane of your arm aligned with your knuckles. Keep the wrist of your lower hand straight, in alignment with your arm. (See chapter 7, SUP Fitness, Injury Prevention, and Cross-Training for more info on holding the paddle).

Never let go of your paddle when you fall. If you do, get back on the board first, then retrieve your paddle.

STANDING UP

Start out by placing the board in water deep enough to prevent the fin from hitting the bottom. Attach the leash to your ankle, and while holding the paddle, walk the board into about 4–5 feet of water—deeper water will cushion your body in case of a fall and will protect the fin. Pick a less crowded area to start.

Climb onto the middle of the board, your body facing down. Once on the deck, twist around toward the nose and straddle the board with both legs. Move yourself back and forth down the length of the board until you feel a good balance position. Ideally you should be in the middle of the board.

If you need to paddle to another location on the water to practice, kneeling or sitting are good positions for beginners and advanced paddlers alike. You can also lie flat on the board with your paddle blade underneath your body and the shaft and handle facing the nose. With both arms over the rails, paddle with your hands to your desired location. Paddling prone can be exhausting if you're not used to it, so don't plan on using this method for long distances unless you have prior experience or are in good shape. Some boards are so wide that you might not be able to reach the water with both hands while lying chest down.

When you're ready to try standing, get on all fours in the middle of the board with your hands flat and evenly spaced and with your paddle in your hands placed horizontally across the deck of the board. Slowly put one foot on the board and then the other, staying low in a squatting position. Your feet should be about a foot apart and facing forward toward the nose of the board.

As you stand up, always keep your knees slightly bent to allow a lower center of gravity and to act as shock absorbers in bumpy water.

> **TIP:** You can practice the method used for standing up on land prior to practicing on water. If on sand, draw an outline of the board. Follow the steps above and repeat a few times until you're comfortable, then try on water.

Standing up

The forward stroke

If you feel a little tippy, widen the distance between your feet, or take a few little strokes. Momentum will help make the board feel more stable. An old saying in kayaking is, "When in doubt, paddle." If you continue to feel unstable, stick with the kneeling or sitting position for a while until you gain your balance and get more comfortable on the board.

BASIC STROKES

Stand up paddleboards are so large that they can be difficult to control without specific strokes. The following section will teach you several different ways to paddle forward and to turn, while keeping your board balanced in both calm and rough water. Many of the strokes require using your torso and core strength, adding much greater stability, flexibility, and power to your paddling.

THE FORWARD STROKE

With your knees slightly bent, dip the paddle in the water on one side about 2 to 3 feet in front of your feet with the angled blade facing away from you. The starting position for your stroke is called the catch.

Sitting and kneeling on the board

Don't pull the blade back until it's in the water. Pull the blade gently in a straight line parallel to the board, being careful not to hit the rails. As you pull, your torso should twist slightly, adding power to your stroke. Pull the blade out just past your feet. As you move the blade forward to your starting position, twist your lower wrist forward to feather the blade, which reduces wind resistance and makes you more efficient. Place the blade back in your starting position again for another stroke. Some paddlers imagine the movement of paddling as pulling the board past the paddle as if the paddle were a stationary object.

> **TIP:** Make sure you remove the paddle a few inches past your feet. Any further and the paddle will lift water like a shovel, thus slowing you down. Also try to reduce splashing on the catch and exit of the blade in the water. Practice slowly first to refine the technique.

After a few strokes on each side you'll notice that the board might want to turn to the opposite side you're paddling on. Switch sides and repeat the stroke on the opposite side.

BRACING

Feeling wobbly? Using the paddle to brace is a great way to regain your balance.

While keeping your feet facing forward, twist your upper body 90 degrees to the unstable side, rotating your lower wrist back to place a portion of the paddle blade face gently on the water surface 2 to 3 feet from your board. You can add pressure to the paddle if needed by pushing down with your lower hand on the paddle shaft. This is called a static brace. Much like an outrigger, this extension of the paddle will help you regain balance. I also use the brace to balance myself while looking around or behind me. You can also use the sweeping brace. In the same body position as used for the static brace, sweep the powerface over the surface of the water to support yourself. This works well while moving.

If you fall despite using a brace, relax and let yourself fall. You can injure your shoulder if you struggle against a forceful brace. Dislocated shoulders from poor bracing are very common, especially in fast-moving current or surf. Remember to hold onto your paddle when falling.

> **TIP:** Dress for the water temperature. You'll have more fun and learn more if you're not afraid to fall into the water.

STAYING STRAIGHT

The easiest way for beginners to paddle straight ahead is to alternate paddling a few strokes on both sides. When you begin to turn, you can paddle on the opposite side for a few strokes. Looking in the direction you're going, rather than at the board, will help keep the board going straight.

Make sure you hold the paddle as vertically as possible and bring it parallel to and as close to the rail as possible. This will help the board stay straight.

Another method is to push down gently with one foot to lower the rail into the water, then paddle on that side only. Try this to find out what happens. Move your stance slightly up and down the board to find the position where this method works best. This is called "adjusting the trim" on the board. If you're too far forward or back, the board will turn harshly instead of going straight. Shorter boards with more rocker are harder to keep straight.

Every board is different, thus each will have a different response in the water, so have fun and experiment to find out what works best for your board. Try different boards to see how each reacts to different techniques.

If you try the above methods and the board is still turning sharply, try a larger fin.

TURNING—REVERSE SWEEP STROKE

To turn right, keep your feet facing forward and twist your torso 90 degrees to the right side. Bend your knees even more to lower your center of gravity. Place the paddle in the water behind you and a few feet away from the board.

While keeping your lower arm nearly straight, untwist your torso to pull your arms and paddle in an arcing direction forward through the water. Pull the blade out

> **TIP:** The more your knees are bent, the easier the board will turn. Bending your knees lowers your center of gravity and makes you more stable.

of the water about a foot from your board. This movement will spin the tail of your board away from your paddle, thus turning the nose to the right. Continue this stroke until you have achieved your desired angle. If you watch the blade throughout the entire stroke, you will turn more efficiently.

If you step both feet backwards toward the tail of the board, you'll find that turning is easier, but you may feel less stable. You can also step one foot ahead of the other, which will also feel unsettling at first but will help turn the board. Stepping forward or backward on the board may feel unstable but it's good practice. To practice, turn in a complete circle, and then try from the opposite side.

TURNING—FORWARD SWEEP STROKE

This is the same as the reverse sweep stroke, but instead you start by placing the paddle ahead of you. If you want to turn left, bend your knees and place the paddle on the right side of the board's nose and twist your torso to the right, keeping your lower arm straight, arcing the paddle around you, and removing the paddle by the tail. Keep turning until you reach your desired direction. Try this on both sides. Watch the blade for best results.

The proper stance for the forward and reverse sweep stroke

TURNING—MIXING THE FORWARD AND REVERSE SWEEPS

Another method of turning involves starting with a reverse sweep on one side, then finishing with a forward sweep on the other side. To turn right, start with a reverse sweep stroke on the right, then place the paddle on the left side in front of you to do a forward sweep. Again, bending your knees to a nearly squatting position will make you more stable and help turn the board quicker. Watching the blade throughout the entirety of each stroke will help turn the board easier.

STOPPING

If you need to stop quickly, you'll need to do several short and quick reverse sweep strokes on both sides.

Twist your torso to one side of the board. Place the paddle behind your feet and with your lower arm straight, rotate forward, untwisting your torso. Pull the blade out just beyond your feet. Repeat on the opposite side until you stop. You should be able to stop in two or three strokes.

You can also slow the board by twisting your torso to place the blade face flat on the water on either side of the tail. Push down on the shaft with your lower arm, which should be straight. The more pressure you apply to the blade, the more resistance or drag you create to slow the board.

If you're in danger of colliding with another paddler or an obstruction, and the above techniques don't work, jump off the board to slow your forward pace. Make sure you hold on to your board and paddle.

ADVANCED STROKES

Advanced strokes require better balance on the board, but they will allow you to move your board more efficiently through the water with less effort.

THE TAHITIAN STROKE

This forward stroke is a very efficient method often used in racing because it can move the board very quickly. Using the forward paddling stance, place your paddle in the water as far forward as you can reach. While keeping your upper arm straight, twist your torso and pull the blade along the rail toward you, removing it before it passes the front of your feet. Feather the blade as you return it to the catch to reduce wind resistence. Do short quick strokes.

J-STROKE

To use this forward stroke method, which comes from canoeing and helps keep the board going straight, start the paddle stroke by the nose of the board. Pull the blade toward you, parallel to the rails. As the blade begins to pass your feet, rotate the blade away from the board by twisting your wrists outward, finishing 2 feet past your feet. To make this stroke more effective, push the rail on the side you're paddling, releasing it as you rewind for the next stroke. Try on both sides.

Some use the J-stroke by starting the "J" at the nose. I find this useful in keeping a short board with a lot of rocker straight: Place the blade face 2 feet away from the nose and pull down past the rail.

SIDE DRAW

The side draw pulls the board sideways to a dock, or helps to catch a wave peak only a few feet away.

Using the same body position as for the brace (see above), turn your torso to one side, keeping your feet forward. Reach out with both arms over the water and place the blade in the water about 2 feet away from the rail with the inside of the blade facing the board.

Pull the paddle toward you, keeping the shaft as vertical as possible, pulling to a few inches from your rail, then rotate the lower wrist forward to release the blade. Return to the starting position by slicing the blade through the water. Rotate your wrist to the normal position and pull the paddle toward you again.

The board will move easier if you lower the rail slightly into the water on the side that you're paddling on. You can move the board diagonally by placing the blade in the water ahead or behind the middle of the board and pulling it toward you. Each board will react differently with this stroke.

NOSE RUDDER

The nose rudder is very effective for turning the board's nose while in moving water.

To turn to the right, take a few strokes to get the board moving forward. Bend your

knees and place the blade about a foot or two to the right of the nose in a neutral position. Your lower arm should be straight. Then rotate your wrists backwards so the

Nose rudder

Sculling brace

inside of the blade faces slightly forward. This will turn the nose of the board to the right. The more angle you use, the more the nose will turn. The faster you are moving, the less angle you'll need to turn the board. Try on both sides. This is a great turn for going around buoys in races.

SCULLING BRACE

This brace works by slowly moving the face of the blade back and forth on or near the surface of the water in a continious side-to-side motion, thus gaining stability by using more water than the static brace. The technique is also referred to as "sculling for support."

While keeping your feet facing the nose, turn your torso 90 degrees to the side you need to brace on. Place the top half of the blade face slightly in the water a few feet from the rail. Using a gentle, continuous side-to-forward torso rotation and cocking your wrists forward and back, move the blade side-to-side, planing on or just below the surface of the water while simultaneously pushing down on the shaft with your lower arm. The revolving blade on the surface should provide lift on the surface of the water.

SCULLING DRAW

This stroke moves the board sideways using the sculling movement. Start with a sculling brace but apply more pressure on your lower arm. This should move your board to one side.

TAIL RUDDER OR PRY

This is a classic rudder stroke often used in canoes on rivers or with outriggers and kayaks in the surf to steer and turn by placing the paddle by the tail while moving.

To turn right while moving forward, bend your knees and twist your torso to the right while keeping your feet facing forward. Extend your lower arm straight out and place the paddle beside the tail. Push the paddle away from the board by twisting your torso to the left. The more you push the paddle out, the more the board turns. Try varying the blade depth to determine how much the board turns. Also try lowering your inside rail, then your outside rail, to see if this increases your turn. Try on both sides.

CROSS BOW PADDLING

This forward stroke/turning technique allows you to paddle on both sides of the board without having to switch hands. It's particularly beneficial in rough water where the time it takes to change hands costs you valuable time in catching a wave or an eddy.

Start on the left side of your board with a forward stroke. At the catch, move the blade across the nose of your board and place it in the water on your right side. Try to take a stroke or do a forward sweep turn or nose rudder while underway. It will feel odd at first, but with practice you'll become comfortable with it.

DUFEK

The dufek originated in whitewater kayaking. It's essentially a static side draw that only works when the board is moving forward or in fast-moving current. I've found it useful in stand up paddling in the surf to move sideways quickly while paddling out. You can also use it to turn a moving board without having to take a stroke. In fast-moving tidal rapids or a river, the dufek can be used to help ferry the board across the current without having to paddle.

To move to the right, take a few forward strokes to get the board moving. While keeping your feet forward, twist your torso to the right side. Using the same arm technique as the side draw (see above), place your paddle vertically in the water 1 to 2 feet from the rail. Cock your wrists back, exposing the inside of the paddle blade to your rail and slightly forward. Hold the

Dufek turn

paddle in this position and watch as the board slides to your right.

Rotate your wrists slightly forward and backward to find which position moves the board best. The more cocked your wrists are, the more the board will want to turn. The more neutral your wrists are, the more the board will go sideways.

Fast-moving current or strong forward momentum will make this stroke more effective. Play with different blade angles and try both sides to see what works best.

PIVOT TURN

The pivot turn is recommended for turning the board 180 degrees very quickly, but it requires good balance. Step both feet toward the rear of the board, or place one foot near the tail so that the nose rises above the water a bit. Make a forward or reverse sweep stroke, turning your torso, to turn the board. You should be able to turn it 180 degrees in one stroke. Lean forward when the nose rises out of the water to maintain stability.

TIP: If you stand back on your board toward the tail, which forces the nose out of the water, the board will turn much easier, as there will be less board in the water to create resistance. This requires more balance, but is good practice. For fun, try to stand as far back as you can, dipping the entire tail in the water, then recover to your normal stance in the middle of the board. Then try this by moving all the way forward on your board, thus raising the tail out of the water. Then return to the board's center.

MIXED STROKES

Just having your paddle in the water adds stability to your board. If you're in a rough water situation, one way to remain stable while turning is to slide the blade face in the water forward along your rail back to the catch. For example, do a forward sweep stroke on your right side. As you finish the stroke, you will be watching your blade, which should be parallel to the rail of your board near the tail with your outer lower arm fully extended. Without removing the blade from the water and still keeping it parallel to your rail, drive your extended

Pivot turn

arm down toward your knees and forward, which will push the blade through the water along your rail until it reaches the catch.

NOSE RUDDER TO DUFEK

If you lose turning momentum while using the nose rudder but are still moving, slide the paddle in the water parallel to your board to the middle. Rotate your wrists and torso away from the board so the blade is at a 45-degree angle facing the nose. If you're still moving, the board will continue to turn as the paddle is acting as a fulcrum,

catching remaining incoming water. Once you've lost momentum, you can untwist your torso and wrists toward the board, then back again in mini strokes to continue turning the board. Keeping a low profile will give you more stability and turn the board more quickly.

TAIL RUDDER TO DUFEK

When the board is moving, twist your torso to the right, extending your lower arm, and drop the blade by your tail with the blade face toward the board. When you begin to lose mo-

Cross bow

mentum, pull the blade in the water parallel to the rail toward to the middle and rotate your wrists and torso out and away from the board. The board should turn to the right.

CROSS BOW TO DUFEK

This stroke turns the board very quickly while at a standstill or while moving. Take a few strokes to gain speed on your right side. Rotate your torso to the left and place the blade in the water on the left side of the board by your toes. The blade should be facing the nose. You may have to bend your knees more for stability and torso rotation. This is a static stroke where the blade stays in one position as the board turns. The board should turn to the left rather quickly.

TIP: Some of the mixed strokes are easier if you slide the blade through the water alongside the rail with the powerface facing the board in between each stroke. For the tail rudder to dufek, slide the blade along the rail from the tail to the middle of the board to do the dufek.

If you're starting out without forward momentum and want to turn more, push the blade forward with both hands, then release it by rotating your wrists toward the board and slice the blade back toward your feet. Rotate your wrists back again to push the blade forward. These mini strokes can turn the nose of the board.

EDGING

While the board is moving forward, dip your right rail, in the water by applying pressure to the rail, and notice the board turning slightly in that direction. Try this again on your left side. This is called edging, a common technique in kayaking. Add a sweep stroke while edging on the same side, and you'll turn the board even more. Try edging on one side and applying a sweep stroke to the opposite side. See what happens. Edging is an important skill that will benefit you in river paddling and surfing. Add edging to all your turning and sculling strokes for efficiency in turning.

CHAPTER 3

Paddlers at Deception Pass State Park, Washington

Flatwater Paddling

Recently a sea kayaker looked at my stand up board and asked, "What's the purpose of that?" I pointed to his sea kayak and said that the SUP is the same as his kayak, just that you stand up. The beauty of the SUP is that for such a simple craft, there are so many ways of getting on the water with it. While the recent reincarnation of SUPs was sparked by surfers seeking better access to more waves, many people have found that stand up paddling is also an excellent way to travel on flatwater.

In 2009, Ken Campbell, a Tacoma, Washington-based kayak guide, paddled his 12-foot SUP 150 miles throughout Puget Sound as a fundraiser for the Washington Water Trails Association (WWTA). The trip took four and a half days. He carried thirty-five pounds of overnight camping gear on the nose of his board and spent several nights along the shores of Puget Sound using WWTA sites.

A year earlier, Dave Collins paddled his 12-foot SUP around the northern tip of Vancouver Island on a 100-kilometer trip. He said that the advantage of using a SUP over a sea kayak on this sort of trip was the increased ability to view wildlife while standing up, and being able to surf waves with a more flexible craft than a kayak. He also said that while 12-foot SUPs are slower than sea kayaks, they do allow full body exercise, which is beneficial for paddlers who might get back pain from sitting in a kayak for long periods of time. You can also paddle while sitting on a SUP, allowing for more flexibility and comfort in varying conditions.

In April of 2010, Jenny Kalmbach and Morgan Hoesterey paddled over 250 miles from the Big Island of Hawaii to Kauai, crossing nine open ocean channels, each with a distinctive personality. The epic, boat-supported trip included a one-night

Dave Collins paddling around the north end of Vancouver Island, British Columbia

paddle crossing from Oahu to Kauai, and a route that passed the tallest cliffs in the world on the north shore of Molokai. Average paddling distances were 20 to 30 miles a day.

In Seattle, I paddle 2–4 miles a day, several days a week on Puget Sound or in the lakes within the city, enjoying city views, local wildlife, and getting a great workout. Inland lakes and waterways are not always flat, and can offer fun surfing opportunities caused by wind or boat wakes. I regularly surf large freighter waves, which can change a quiet flatwater paddle into an exciting surfing session hours from the ocean.

It's common for paddlers to perceive flatwater as easy paddling. It's also common for people to see SUPs as so stable and easy to use that they think less gear and clothing are necessary. As with any type of paddle adventure, stand up paddling on flatwater requires thorough planning.

ADVANCE PLANNING

To avoid being caught in bad weather or an uncomfortable situation on the water, plan ahead and stay within your skill level. Check the weather prior to leaving. If the barometer is dropping or rising rapidly, a change is expected within a few hours. You should also paddle with a friend, preferably a more experienced paddler, on your first trips out. Dress for the water temperature, and bring extra water to drink, particularly in warmer climates or in summer. Bring more water than you think you need. Always wear your PFD and leash. If you're paddling at night or coming back at dusk, bring a waterproof light. Also bring a cell phone and/or VHF radio in waterproof bags.

There are several easy ways to determine whether you should go out or not. As a beginner, it's best to avoid windy days until you have improved your strength and balance to be comfortable in rough conditions.

TIPS FOR PLANNING YOUR PADDLE:
- Stay within your skill level.
- Make a float plan; tell others where you're going and for how long.
- Always paddle with a friend.
- Check the weather prior to leaving.
- Dress for the water temperature.
- Bring water or electrolyte replacement drinks to prevent dehydration.
- Always wear your leash.
- Wear your PFD, and pack it with flares, knife, energy bar or gels, and whistle.
- Consider bringing a backup break-down SUP or kayak paddle.
- Bring a waterproof light in case you come back after dark.
- Consider carrying a VHF radio and/or cell phone in a waterproof case.
- Be willing to cancel if the weather and conditions are above your skill level.

PREDICTING WEATHER

Most accidents on the water occur due to weather-related incidents. There are several easy ways to check on weather in advance.

- Using local, real-time data websites such as National Oceanic and Atmospheric Association (NOAA), check current wind speed and direction, air temperature, water temperature, swell size, and pressure levels.
- Find a local webcam that covers the area you plan on paddling. Check to see how often it updates to make sure the image is current.
- Check forecasts on a weather radio or VHF radio. These are broadcast from the National Weather Service and are current. If you're using radios on the water, carry them in a waterproof bag and bring extra batteries.
- Look outside to see what the weather is doing. Is the wind picking up? What direction is the wind going? Are clouds moving in? How much are the bushes swaying? Are there small tree branches breaking? Also look at animals signs. Are the cows sitting? Are birds huddled together? Are the seagulls flying inland?
- Use an electronic device such as an iPhone or BlackBerry that has apps designed to forecast weather or surf forecasts. Use a product-specific waterproof bag or make your own, and carry extra batteries.
- Stop by the location where you plan to put in. Too choppy? Is there protection from the wind?

- If you have a barometer on your watch or wall, or have access to a website such as NOAA, check the pressure readings. If it's dropping or rising rapidly, expect bad weather soon. If it's steady, expect no change. The barometer is one of the more reliable sources of weather information.

> **TIP: Don't trust seven-day forecasts! No one can accurately predict weather or ocean swell reports more than two or three days out.**

WEATHER HAZARDS

Wind vs. current. Large, confused waves can be created when wind opposes current. If you're not comfortable with rough-water paddling or surfing, keep an eye out for such conditions. River mouths are a common location for this effect. The Elwha River mouth in Washington State is known for large, steep, and fast hollow waves due to the outgoing river current, which jacks up incoming ocean swell; it's not an area for beginners. In shallow areas, large waves can develop and make for difficult paddling if you're not experienced in such conditions.

High wind. Wind above 15 knots can make paddling difficult if going upwind. Whitecaps occur at 17–21 knots when the wind begins to build small breaking waves on the water. These waves are big enough to topple beginner paddlers. Winds above

High wind day

25 knots can make large waves that only experienced paddlers should attempt.

Lightning. If you see a dark rain cloud adjacent to blue skies, expect lightning, which can put you in a very dangerous position. If you're already on the water, seek shelter immediately.

Wind. Even the slightest amount of wind can blow your board out of your reach after a fall, especially if you aren't wearing a leash. Paddling upwind on a SUP can be very difficult if you are not in shape or if the wind is quite strong. If you are new to stand up paddling or are alone, don't go out in very windy conditions. Pay attention to the direction you're paddling to avoid having to paddle upwind to get home. Paddlers who race like to paddle against the wind for training.

Fetch. Fetch is an effect of wind that has blown over a long distance of water, building large waves. Large lakes or similar bodies of water can build ocean-sized waves, a hazard or a benefit depending on your paddling experience. On Puget Sound, I'll wait until a 20-knot or greater wind blows nearly three hours, then go look for waves to surf in certain locations. In this period of time, water can go from flat to frothing with 4-foot breaking waves. Ocean swell is created with fetch due to large storms thousands of miles from where the waves might end up.

Beam seas. These are waves created by side winds. They can lead to tricky paddling because the side wind may push you off course. Paddle on the opposite side to counter the wind's effect on your board.

Quartering seas. These are wind-driven waves that come from an angle toward your board.

Following seas. Following seas are created by wind pushing from behind you. To a beginner this might be uncomfortable, but for experienced paddlers following seas give them a free ride to their destination, and might even create breaking waves. Downwinders (see below) are done on following seas.

DOWNWINDERS

Downwinders are very popular among stand up paddlers. The term refers to paddling downwind for long distances on big wind days, when large, surfable waves are present due to fetch. In coastal areas, swell goes either in the direction of the wind, or against it, making the waves even bigger, depending on the area. Paddlers in Hawaii have reported downwind swells up to 20 feet, and surfing and paddling speeds up to 14 mph. The popular Maliko run on Maui is known for huge swells and surf. For those in inland locations, downwinders can be found on lakes and big rivers, giving you a surfing experience far from the ocean. You don't have to have 20-foot ocean swells to have a good time. I've been paddling in wind for years and enjoy any push or free ride I can get.

In choosing a route or location to do a downwinder, make sure your paddling skills are suitable for the location and conditions. For example, don't think about trying a downwinder in a coastal area if you've never surfed before. And high wind paddling isn't the same as a glassy day of surfing. Wind

> **TIP: Find local resources that give historical weather information for your region. For example, if May tends to be wet and windy with strong winds from the south, then perhaps May isn't the best month for you to go. NOAA has such information.**

Mark Raaphorst on a downwinder

BEAUFORT WIND SCALE

Developed in 1805 by Sir Francis Beaufort of England

Force	Wind (Knots)	WMO Classification	Appearance of Wind Effects	
			On the Water	On Land
0	Less than 1	Calm	Sea surface smooth and mirror-like	Calm, smoke rises vertically
1	1–3	Light air	Scaly ripples, no foam crests	Smoke drift indicates wind direction, still wind vanes
2	4–6	Light breeze	Small wavelets, crests glassy, no breaking	Wind felt on face, leaves rustle, vanes begin to move
3	7–10	Gentle breeze	Large wavelets, crests begin to break, scattered whitecaps	Leaves and small twigs constantly moving, light flags extended
4	11–16	Moderate breeze	Small waves 1–4 feet becoming longer, numerous whitecaps	Dust, leaves, and loose paper lifted, small tree branches move
5	17–21	Fresh breeze	Moderate waves 4–8 feet taking longer form, many whitecaps, some spray	Small trees in leaf begin to sway
6	22–27	Strong breeze	Larger waves 8–13 feet, whitecaps common, more spray	Larger tree branches moving, whistling in wires
7	28–33	Near gale	Sea heaps up, waves 13–20 feet, white foam streaks off breakers	Whole trees moving, resistance felt walking against wind
8	34–40	Gale	Moderately high (13–20 feet) waves of greater length, edges of crests begin to break into spindrift, foam blown in streaks	Whole trees in motion, resistance felt walking against wind
9	41–47	Strong gale	High waves (20 feet), sea begins to roll, dense streaks of foam, spray may reduce visibility	Slight structural damage occurs, slate blows off roofs
10	48–55	Storm	Very high waves (20–30 feet) with overhanging crests, sea white with densely blown foam, heavy rolling, lowered visibility	Seldom experienced on land, trees broken and uprooted, considerable structural damage
11	56–63	Violent storm	Exceptionally high (30–45 feet) waves, foam patches cover sea, visibility more reduced	
12	64+	Hurricane	Air filled with foam, waves over 45 feet, sea completely white with driving spray, visibility greatly reduced	

waves can be chaotic with very small periods between each wave. In some cases, if you let go of your paddle, it'll take off ahead of you and possibly out of reach. Do you have a backup paddle? If you fall, can you get back up in rough water? Thirty knots of wind is considered a gale. The Beaufort Scale describes forty knots as follows: "Difficult to control your boat. Makes rescues and communication difficult." Make sure you can recognize your take-out and can make it there. What if you can't? Do you have a secondary take-out location?

Also make sure you wear your leash and carry extra water for hydration. A VHF radio could be a benefit in coastal areas where you'll be far from shore. My rule of thumb in rough water paddling is to have fun, but to stay off the evening news. Always paddle with others, especially those that are comfortable or more experienced than you in high wind paddling, surf, and rough water.

Longer boards are best in downwinders because they make it easier to catch waves on smaller days or to keep up with the swell on big coastal days. Longer boards will also give you more stability if the water is rough and you're new to such paddling.

UPWIND PADDLING

Paddling upwind on a SUP is a lot of work, and can be difficult if you have a long way to go and hadn't planned for the extra effort. Headwinds come directly at you, often creating waves to paddle against. By sitting with your legs crossed, out front, or

> **TIP: Use Water Safety Hand Signals (see Chapter 5, River and Tidal Rapids Paddling) to communicate when the wind and waves make it hard to hear.**

kneeling, you can cut wind resistance and make better forward progress. When sitting, hold one hand just above the blade, and the other 1–2 feet higher on the shaft. Keep your lower arm nearly straight, which forces you to use your torso for power and to save strength in your arms. Try sitting on different positions on the board to see what works best for balance, and for cutting through incoming waves and wind. You might consider carrying a two-piece break-down kayak paddle for upwinders. Paddling prone is also an effective way to paddle upwind. Paddling in a zigzag route upwind puts your body sideways to the wind, making you more efficient.

PADDLING IN THE LEE OF THE WIND

If you're seeking a location to paddle on a windy day but don't want to get in rough water, look for calm water in the "lee" of the wind. This term reflects an area of water protected from the wind, usually caused by a large land mass. Where I usually paddle, if it's blowing 20 knots plus from the south, I look for an area of water on the north side of a hill. Often marinas and docks create calm sections of water that allow for a mellow paddle on a stormy day. You can also use these sections of calm water to take a break or find safety during a storm.

DRIFT

When paddling in the wind, pay attention to your drift to determine if the wind is pushing you away from your planned destination or into a rougher section of water you would like to avoid. Once, when I was paddling along a shoreline on the way home, strong side winds and an outgoing tide in the direction of the wind pushed me seaward and made forward paddling

> **TIP: If you don't want to surf in to a beach, wait for a lull between wave sets, then paddle in. If a wave comes, let it go under you, then gain speed to paddle in on the backside of the wave.**

difficult. I compensated by paddling more on the side from which the wind was coming. Edging or dropping a rail might assist in keeping you on track as well. Side winds are also called beam winds.

TIDES

Tides are changes in sea level created by the gravitational force between the earth, sun, and moon. Tides are more extreme during periods of the full and new moon. At these times the sun, the earth, and the moon are aligned, creating a strong gravitational force. At quarter moon, the sun and the moon exert gravitational pulls at right angles, which dilutes the overall effect. Depending on the configuration of the local ocean basin and adjacent land masses, tides are more extreme in some parts of the world than in others.

In most parts of the world, the high-low tidal cycle lasts approximately twelve

UNDERSTANDING TIDAL CYCLES

Ebb – outgoing tide

Flood – incoming tide

Slack – in between ebb and flood

Tidal Current Chart – map of an area with arrows showing the direction of the currents through inlets and around islands at either ebb or flood. Some tidal charts list the minimum and maximum current in any certain area for daily tidal exchanges

Tide Table – shows hourly changes in tidal heights

Currents Table – shows hourly changes in current speeds and directions.

Reverse Current – where current flows in different directions around an island or similar location hours. The tide will rise for six hours, then fall for six hours, resulting in two high and two low tides in a 24-hour period. Currents correspond to this cycle also. The current will flood for six hours, then reverse and ebb for six hours.

TRAINING

If you're planning an extended trip on your SUP, make sure you're competent in the type of water you'll be paddling in. If you're going to be in a surf zone, for example, make sure you can paddle out and surf comfortably in through waves with a loaded board. Surfing is a great way to increase your overall skill level and confidence in any type of water. Practice paddling in wind, particularly upwind, which is a great workout. Since nature is rarely consistent, also paddle in side winds. You'll paddle one side longer than you're used to and learn to control your board in such conditions. Are you comfortable climbing back on your board in 20 knots plus of wind in rough breaking seas?

A loaded board will be slower than what you might be used to and will require you to stand back further to compensate for the weight on the front. You should practice paddling a few miles with a load similar to the one you'll be carrying on your trip. This will give you a chance to test if the tie-downs work and whether the load will shift. Go on a "shakedown" overnight trip prior to leaving on a longer trip. Bring everything you're planning on carrying, and everyone, for that matter. If there are any gear or personality issues with your group, it's better to find out close to home than halfway around the world.

GEAR

A well outfitted board makes expedition paddling easier and safer. Over the years I have learned some simple solutions that have served me well on longer trips. For example, you can attach raft plugs to the board with marine glue in order to strap nylon rope or bungees to hold down gear. EZ Plugs can be attached to the board with marine epoxy. NSI makes a fabric loop that is attached to the board using a peel-stick adhesive. If you have a soft top or deck pad on the nose of your board, carefully remove that material in the shape of your plug, clean with alcohol, sand to create texture, then apply the plug. Make sure you allow the epoxy to cure long enough. Have a shaper install leash plugs to your board to get the most secure method of attaching a load.

Motorcycle netting is a great option to attach to the nylon rope or bungee tie-downs on your board. The netting will hold your gear tighter and prevent smaller items from slipping out.

Consider packing your gear into two dry bags to ensure dryness. Waterproofed kayak deck bags are also useful for holding gear. Deck bags have plastic clips that can be secured to your tie-down ropes to prevent slippage or loss in rough seas

Ken Campbell paddling with a full load on Puget Sound (Photo by Corinne Miller)

or surf. Make sure your load is balanced prior to leaving and that it won't slide from side to side.

Carry your board to the beach first, then haul your gear down. Lightweight mesh backpacks and duffel bags are available to assist in hauling dry bags and other gear to your board. These are also helpful in carrying your gear from your board to your campsite, saving you a few trips after a long paddle.

BOARDS

For touring and extended trips, the longer the board, the faster you'll go. You can also carry more gear. Compromises must be made when choosing a board for trips. If you want to surf in hard-to-reach locations that require a long paddle, you might want a shorter board for more fun on the waves. If you don't plan on surfing and are going considerable distances, then longer is better. The first SUPs available resembled large surfing boards, but weren't necessarily designed for flatwater long distance paddling and efficiency. Recently, board designers have begun to offer designs with kayak-like hulls and bows/noses that can cut through water easier and faster.

Inflatable Boards

While slower than fiberglass boards, inflatable SUPs can roll up and travel anywhere, making them ideal for international travel. Traditional fiberglass SUPs can be very expensive to ship, and they are vulnerable to damage.

Quality inflatables are very stiff when fully inflated, and can surf well and travel distances efficiently. In rugged environments such as rivers or outer coastal areas, inflatables hold up fairly well to hard or sharp surfaces.

According to expedition paddler Dave Collins, raft plugs don't attach well to the thick rubber material on inflatable boards, so he wraps rope around the board to secure his load to the deck. While he admits there might be some drag, it's not enough to affect overall speed.

PADDLES

Use a longer paddle for paddling distances. Ken Campbell (see sidebar), for example, is more than six feet tall and prefers an 85-inch-long paddle, but feels he could go longer. He also straps a two- or three-piece break-down kayak paddle to his board's nose, which is more efficient when paddling upwind in a sitting position. Ken suggests using a three-piece paddle because it packs down smaller and doesn't get in the way of your feet while you're paddling.

PACKING FOR TRIPS

Packing efficiently and as lightly as possible is essential for overnight trips on a SUP. Here are a few suggestions based on my own experiences over the years.

Down sleeping bag. Some say down is a poor choice in wet environments because it won't keep you warm when wet. But down packs much smaller and is lighter than synthetic filling, and if you use two dry bags you should be able to keep a down bag dry.

Pillow. There are several inflatable pillows available that pack very small. I've never found stuffing my own clothing into a stuff sack to be very comfortable, but lots of people do.

Silk sleeping bag liner. Sleeping bag liners are lightweight and will increase your bag's temperature rating by at least 10 degrees. They also offer your body a comfy rather than clammy feeling inside the bag. In warmer climates, liners may be a cooler replacement for a sleeping bag.

Compact inflatable sleeping pad. Inflatable pads pack thinner than closed-cell foam pads, and they offer greater insulation on cold nights. I once forgot my pad on a three-day winter paddle trip during which nighttime temperatures dropped into the 30s. I layered all my clothing and dry bags under my sleeping bag to replace the

KEN CAMPBELL

I first heard of Ken Campbell when I purchased his self-published sea kayak guide, *Shades of Gray,* one in a series of five books by his own Little Bay Press.

In the summer of 2009 the Tacoma, Washington resident paddled 150 miles throughout Puget Sound on his stand up paddleboard as a fundraiser to support the Washington Water Trails Association, an organization that promotes advocacy, education, and stewardship of public access to Washington's waterways for people in human- and wind-powered beachable watercraft. He was the first SUP paddler in the region to take this trip, called the Puget Sound Challenge.

Ken Campbell runs his own sea kayak and SUP instruction and guide service, Azimuth Expeditions. He frequently takes his board on overnight trips, carrying roughly thirty pounds of gear strapped to the nose of his 12-foot 1-inch Laird or Bark 14 Expedition board. He prefers ultra light gear due to the SUP's limited storage space and he admits he has to leave the Dutch oven at home. Ken travels 22 miles a day on average with a loaded board—longer with the assistance of a tailwind or helpful current.

Ken's blog, The Last Wilderness, focuses on the history, politics, and natural history of Washington's Olympic Peninsula. A frequent lecturer, Ken often speaks at sea kayak symposiums and other related public places. Find out more about Ken on his website and blog (http://lastwilderness.blogspot.com/).

pad, but still froze. There are several dry bags available to keep your pad dry while paddling.

Water purifier. If you're paddling in areas where tap or well water isn't available, bring a water purifier to filter microorganisms such as giardia. Bring either a few plastic bottles or a large folding plastic container or bladder to store your filtered water. You can also drop a crystalline iodine tablet in your water to make sure. Boiling your water will also kill most parasites.

Water storage. Whether you need to store your filtered water or carry all your water into a campsite, you'll need reliable storage for it. Cloth or plastic fold-down bladders can carry more than a gallon. Hard plastic containers are not practical as they take up too much space on your board and may cause balance issues. Hydration packs can be attached to your PFD or a backpack for easy drinking while paddling. Flattened two-liter soda pop bottles are a more economical option; they are easy to store and won't roll away.

Stove. Consider using the smallest compact white gas stove you can find. Many manufacturers such as MSR and Primus make efficient self-igniting stoves that pack small yet can boil a pot of water in a few minutes. Still bring your matches or lighter, as the self-igniting feature can fail. I put my stove, lighter, and fuel canisters in a dry bag to prevent saltwater corrosion. A lightweight aluminum silver reflector shield is worth bringing to block wind and help the stove work more efficiently. Bring enough fuel canisters and bring a stove repair kit and extra parts. Butane stoves also work well and are less finicky than white gas stoves, but the butane fuel canisters cannot be recycled.

Pots and pans. Consider using titanium cookware. Although it's quite expensive, it's the lightest metal available. Put items such as tea, coffee, or dried soup packets in the pots while traveling to save space.

Tent. Use a 3-season tent with a rain fly in colder weather. Floorless tents also offer a lighter option. Bring a plastic sheet to go under the tent.

Bivy sack. A waterproof bivy bag can keep you warm and dry in warmer weather if you'd rather not carry a tent. Sleeping bag covers are another no-tent option—or use one to stay warmer inside a tent.

Tarp. A plastic or nylon tarp is a must for rain and wind protection. Put it over your tent to keep it dry, or to create a separate kitchen area. A tarp can also be tied to tree branches to create a makeshift, waterproof shelter. Break-down aluminum center poles are available for use with tarps, but a paddle will suffice. Bring 50 yards of thin nylon cord and a knife to secure the tarp to trees or rocks.

Frameless backpack. A backpack is useful for carrying gear from your board to your campsite or car. It may also come in handy if you have an emergency and have to hike out with all your gear.

Toiletries. Take advantage of the mini travel gear at your local drugstore. I put toilet paper in a ziplock bag. Get biodegradable liquid soap to prevent polluting your campsite or local water sources. Also bring lip balm, sunblock, and a small container of skin cream to protect your face and hands from getting dry and cracked.

Clock. If you need to catch an early morning flood tide, an alarm will be invaluable. Use either your cell phone or a mini travel clock. Be aware that cell phone batteries wear down quickly.

Solar chargers. You can now get affordable small solar chargers that will restore the batteries of your various electronic devices in remote locations. Many of these are very small and won't add much weight to your overall load.

TIP: If you're paddling near the coast, conserve drinking water by using saltwater to brush your teeth. In his book *Sea Kayaker's Savvy Paddler,* Doug Alderson recommends using ⅓ saltwater when cooking pasta. Boil the pasta for half the required time, then let it sit in the water until it softens. Cook rice when you're low on water. Pasta water gets thrown out, but the water used to cook rice is completely absorbed.

Communication. A VHF radio is essential for any remote trip, including mountain or inland coastal trips. Cell phones are good if you have reception, but are not as reliable as a VHF. Satellite phones are reliable, but very expensive.

Helmet. You'll want a helmet with ear protection when paddling in rough coastal conditions or in surf. Many light options are available.

Spare clothes. Think synthetic. In colder temps, cotton doesn't keep you warm, especially when it's wet. Wool, fleece, polypropylene, capilene, and similar fabrics are best. I usually carry one pair of capilene long johns, both top and bottom. A fleece neck gaiter is a smaller alternative to a scarf. If paddling in warmer climates, bring along a light coat in case the nights get cool. Store a fresh bag of clothes in your car to change into at the end of your trip. In warmer climates, lighter colored UV-protective clothing will keep you cooler with more protection from the sun. Hawaiian long-distance paddler Jenny Kalmbach recommends a good hat, sunglasses, sunscreen, a long sleeve top, paddling gloves, and shoes or booties. She also uses 2XU compression tights, which keep the blood flowing so your muscles get fresh oxygenated blood.

Fishing gear. If you like to fish, bring along a telescoping pole or hand line. A friend of mine carries a small packable crab pot that flattens on his board when not in use. Check local fishing regulations prior to leaving. In summer watch out for red tide or similar warnings that will close most fishing areas. (see Fishing below).

Mesh nylon bag. Keep your beer or perishable food items cold by dipping them in the water near your camp. In Puget Sound, the water is 45 to 60 degrees all year, great for keeping things cool. I attach a nylon rope to the bag, which I have tied to a rock or log on shore. Throw the bag out so it sinks down a few feet. Watch the tides to make sure the rope tied to the log isn't submerged after you wake from an afternoon nap.

Food. Keep your cooking simple to reduce weight. While freeze dried foods might not be your top choice for flavor, they are light and require only a small amount of hot water.

Use saltwater to clean your kitchen utensils, pots, and pans. Fold-down fabric kitchen sink bags are available.

TIP: Set up your tent, tarp, and other gear prior to your trip to make sure you know how it works. Tarps can be tricky, especially in a downpour or high winds. Practice setting up tarps at home.

Rain gear. Whether paddling in a dry or wet suit, it's a good idea to have nylon or Gore-Tex rain gear to put on over your paddling clothes during breaks, and to stay warm or dry in wet weather. Ponchos are also a good option. There are several very warm Gore-Tex and fleece-lined hats available.

Kitchen items. Hand sanitizer is a must for cleaning after restroom use and prior to eating. Buy a fabric zipper or fold-up bag to carry your basic utensils. Other essential items include a can and bottle opener, which can both be found on multitools; plastic bowl; insulated cup with lid; cutting board; aluminum foil (cut a large piece and fold it to avoid having to carry a roll); paring knife; spatula; and small plastic containers for spices, salt and pepper, and cooking oil. Bring a small sponge and biodegradable kitchen soap.

Rope. Bring a paddler's tow or throw rope for rescues and for hanging your wet gear at camp. It can also be used to haul gear up steep hillsides, to assist in portages, and to hang bags away from bears.

Navigation gear. The well prepared paddler will carry a waterproof watch (on PFD), a marine compass, a hiker's compass, nautical charts and maps in large ziplock bags, a current table, tide tables, a parallel ruler, a waterproof logbook and pencil, a GPS, and a local guidebook.

Thermos. If you're paddling in cold temperatures, there's nothing better than a hot drink or hot soup.

Monocular. Instead of bulky, heavy binoculars, consider a monocular. Small, waterproof models are available. You can use a monocular to spot ships coming from afar, and to look for campsites and landing spots in rough water.

Gear repair kit. In case a tent pole breaks, you find a small leak in your sleeping pad, or your board gets dinged up, bring along a few items for repairs: duct tape, needle and thread, tent sealer (seam sealer), extra tent pole sleeve, multitool, five-minute epoxy, and a carabiner. If you're tying your gear load down with bungee or rope, bring extra in case of a break.

Fire starter. If you're camping in an area where campfires are allowed, bring fire starter in case available wood is wet. You can buy chemical fire starters, or you can make your own. A frugal friend of mine brings small 2x4 scraps, which make great kindling.

Waterproof headlamp or flashlight. Essential item for paddling at night and working with your hands free around camp. Store extra batteries in small plastic containers or film canisters.

NIGHT PADDLING

I often paddle at night on Puget Sound. In winter, a windless, full-moon night shimmering with stars can be quite an experience. During warm summer evenings, I love the eerie and colorful bioluminescent light displays. Each paddle stroke leaves a white swirling cloud of illuminated water behind. Schools of fish and harbor seals dart below my board with psychedelic trails of light.

Night paddling requires that all your senses be fully engaged in the experience. Other boaters won't expect a stand up paddleboard at night. Scan the horizon for moving lights to avoid crossing in front of a powerboat. You should be able to identify different boats by their running lights.

Sailboats have one white light at the top of their mast. Tug boats have three vertical lights above the pilot house. Powerboats usually have one green and one red light. Small dinghies or fishing boats should have one white light. But don't count on lights; in my paddling area there is a guy who regularly speeds through the night on his jet ski, without lights. Listen for boat motors, because some small dinghies and inflatable rafts don't have running lights.

Tugs towing barges often don't light the barge or the long towing cable. Never cross between a tug and its barge. Pay attention to these hazards, which will ruin an otherwise pleasant evening paddle. Pay attention to lights on shore to keep your bearings, but keep in mind that those lights are unreliable. Street lights may be more reliable than a house light, which may turn off late at night.

MAKING YOURSELF AND YOUR GEAR VISIBLE AT NIGHT

There are several easy ways of making yourself visible to other boaters at night, or to alert others of your presence in case of an accident. The Coast Guard requires you to show a white light upon request. To make it easy, I attach a small waterproof LED to the rear of my PFD, fanny pack, or wet suit, which makes me visible from behind. This way the light's illumination doesn't affect my night vision but makes me visible from afar. Bicycle shops sell super bright LED and water-resistant halogen lights that work well for paddling. Blinking lights are illegal in some states. Avoid red and green lights because they may be confused with navigational lights on a boat.

Waterproof headlamps are also a good source of light. LED are the brightest but don't shine very far. They are best for making you visible, and tend to be small and more comfortable. Halogen lights have the longest projection but tend to be bulky. Regardless of what sort of light you use, carry an extra set of batteries.

Another option is to attach a waterproof light to your board using a suction cup. These specialized white lights are several inches tall, rising above your board to make you more visible. Use a safety line attached to your leash cup in case the suction cup fails. Suction cup lights tend to shine 360 degrees.

You can also stick silver reflector tape to the rails and deck of your board. Stick a few pieces to your paddle blade as well. If there's an emergency, you can swing your

JENNY KALMBACH

Costa Rican native and Kona, Hawaii resident Jenny Kalmbach is an elite ocean paddler who made history in 2008 when she competed in and won all seven SUP races that she entered, including the first annual Battle of the Paddle. In 2009 she won the Solo Female title in the Rainbow Sandals Molokai to Oahu Paddleboard Race, which included both SUPs and prone paddleboards, and came in third in the second annual Battle of the Paddle distance race.

(Photo by Gregg Hoesterey)

In April 2010 she and elite SUP paddler Morgan Hoesterey set out on a month-long expedition, which they called "Destination 3°, to cross the three degrees of latitude that separate the islands of Hawaii and the nine channels that link them. Starting from the Big Island and ending on Kauai, they paddled over a total estimated distance of 250 miles, paddling anywhere between 8 to 70 miles a day, and crossing the Oahu–Kauai Channel during the night.

Jenny, a Naish team paddler, embraced the challenge as a once in a lifetime adventure and an opportunity to raise awareness about the impact of plastics contamination in ocean waters for the Algalita Marine Research Foundation (www.algalita.org).

Jenny prepares for endurance trips by spending a lot of time at her local gym with a trainer, focusing on core and balance, and strengthening her lower body. She also likes to do interval training on the treadmill or bike, or by running hills. She says, "It's important for your body to be fit for endurance paddling but a big part of it is your mind as well. You have to stay positive and avoid getting frustrated. It's not always easy to do, but the more you smile when you're out there the more fun you'll have and the faster you'll go!"

You can learn more about Jenny and Morgan's adventure at www.destination3.com.

paddle above you to better attract attention. Many PFDs, backpacks, and fanny packs come with these reflector strips, and you can purchase fabric reflector strips to sew or stick to your clothing or PFD.

Chemical light sticks can also be attached to your PFD, board, or paddle. If you tie a long string to the end of the chemical stick and swing it in a circle, you will be visible from far away.

In addition to a headlamp, carrying a bright LED waterproof flashlight is a good idea. Tie the flashlight on a string attached to your PFD so you don't lose it. Make sure the string is long enough for easy use, but not so long that it could wrap around your neck.

Waterproof laser pointers can be shined into the pilot house of an incoming boat. These are to be used only in an emergency because the laser can cause flash blindness in anyone looking directly at it. Attach with a string to your PFD.

Many SUP paddles are fiberglass or carbon fiber, which is a black material. It's very easy to put your paddle on your board while taking a break and have it slide off and float away. It's happened to most of us. One solution is to wrap white plastic electrical tape or silver reflector tape around the paddle shaft to better spot it in the dark. Make sure you wrap the tape in areas where it won't get in the way of your paddling grip. If you do lose your paddle, shine your flashlight or headlamp to find the paddle.

If you have tie-downs on your board, slide your paddle under the bungees to keep it from slipping off your board during a break. I also use this technique during the day when pulling something out of my PFD or while taking a rest. Don't attach your paddle to your wrist with cord or bungee as this can lead to a hand injury in a fall, and it prevents paddling on both sides.

In areas where there are no lights on shore to mark your bearings, use a marine compass or GPS.

PADDLING WITH BOATS

On hot summer days boats line up for hours at the Ballard Locks in Seattle, and when finally released into the Puget Sound they resemble wild bulls let loose into the streets of Pamplona. Nearby is a public beach from which SUPs and kayaks launch to cross the marked boating channel accessing the Sound. There's usually 1–3 knots of visible current released from the locks that flows down the channel past the beach. Several times I have witnessed novice stand up paddlers crossing the channel without looking upstream toward the incoming boats. On the west side of the channel a shallow shoal extends out nearly 300 yards, giving the motorboats little room to work with. Once I saw a motorboat swerve out of the way of a paddler only to endanger other paddlers coming from two different directions across the channel.

When crossing a busy boating channel, especially if you're not comfortable with rough water or waves, wait for the boats to pass and for their wakes to dissipate, then cross. I've seen many new paddlers hastily cross behind a line of boats, only to be dismounted by boat wake. If there's another boat coming directly behind, you've got a problem. If you're in a group of paddlers, wait for the boats to pass, and cross the channel all at once, minimizing

> **TIP: Whether paddling at night or day, when you take a break and are sitting on your board, put your leg over the shaft of the paddle to keep it from floating away.**

Paddler in busy waterway

your impact. Keep an eye out for slower paddlers in your group.

Many times over the years, I've had powerboats coming toward me at full speed in open water. With their bows up, they were oblivious to anything in front of them. In a small human-powered craft, you have few options.

As much as paddlers may dislike it, boats usually have the right of way over human-powered craft. When paddling in urban areas, you should know the "Rules of the Road," published by the Coast Guard and titled *Navigation Rules*. Also know where the boating and shipping channels are. Ships have right-of-way over paddlers because they are restricted to a specific path. You should always be prepared to yield the right-of-way, because if you don't, you are bound to lose. You do, however, have the right-of-way in some cases. (See next page).

AVOIDING COLLISIONS

If you feel you might be on a head-on collision course with a boater, change your course to starboard (your right). The other boater should do so as well. You'll pass the boat port to port (left side). Make sure your course change to starboard is obvious to the other boater. If you're unsure of right-of-way, try to stay out of the way of vessels larger or faster than you.

Bow-Angle Method

The bow-angle method is a sure way of determining whether you're on a collision course with incoming boaters. When a ship or boat is coming your way, point your paddle or arm toward it and note the angle between your paddle shaft and the front of your board. Continue checking this angle every few minutes as you paddle. If the angle gets smaller (the paddle shaft

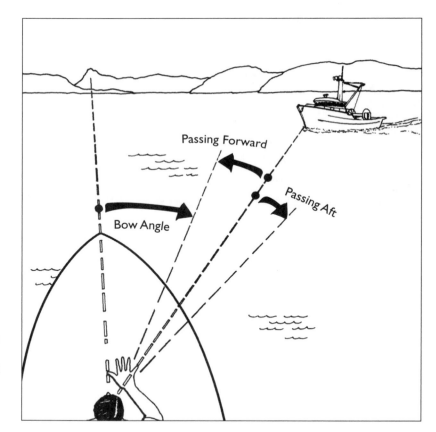

Surfing bow angle method of determining the speed of incoming boats (courtesy of Starpath School of Navigation)

Boats, kayaks, and SUPs share the same waters.

moves closer to the nose of your board), the vessel will pass behind you. If the angle gets larger, it'll pass in front of you. When the angle doesn't change, you're on a collision course. Change your course immediately if a collision is imminent. Keep checking to see if the vessel changes its course.

A similar method involves using your hand and fingers to determine how other vessels will cross your path. For a boat coming toward your left, place your left hand on your board, facing the nose, with your fingers spread out on the deck and your thumb lined up with the center line of the board. Line up one finger with the incoming ship's bow. Use the center of the board as a guide. If the angle increases, the boat will pass behind. If the angle decreases, the boat will pass in front of you. If there's no change in angle, you're on a collision course.

BOB MCDERMOTT

Born in Sacramento, California, Bob McDermott started stand up paddling while living in Hawaii. Now a Seattle resident, Bob was the second stand up paddler I saw on Puget Sound a few years ago. Always surrounded by water, Bob works in the marine industry for a company that repairs yachts. After work he paddles, still wearing his work boots, on nearby lakes, canals, and in Puget Sound, often with his dog on the nose of the board.

Bob loves to race. His favorite is the 13-mile Round the Rock which, being the longest race in the Seattle area, also attracts the highest number of competitors. He said, "It makes me smile to see so many paddleboards at once."

Bob also enjoys strong weather and the abundance of sea life. "On a 32-day Hurricane Island Outward Bound trip, I had an occasion to meet a small bird called a storm petrel. It exists mostly on the waves hunting and breeding in the face of huge storms, flying inches above the swells and breaking waves seemingly oblivious to the tempest all around it. I try to think about the storm petrel when it starts to get a little hairy out there."

OVERTAKING VESSELS

When a vessel is overtaking you from behind, you have the right-of-way, except in shipping lanes where ships always have the right-of-way.

SHIPPING LANES

SUPs have no right-of-way in shipping lanes. Marine charts clearly mark such areas. You can check on your VHF radio to see whether ships are coming your way prior to crossing shipping lanes and to learn the speed and destination of any vessels coming or going. You can call your local area channel to inquire about incoming traffic, as well as to give your position, which will be broadcast to others in the area. Large vessels such as freighters move at nearly 20 knots, and while they may look slow they are moving quite fast. Don't assume you'll clear their path if you make a run for it. Such vessels don't stop for smaller boats.

FERRY BOATS & COMMUTER CRAFT

Ferry boats usually follow a predictable path to and from their destinations; however, they may adjust their course to avoid other marine traffic or marine mammals such as whales. Make sure you know their routes, and either avoid them or make a quick crossing only after a ferry has passed. Make a note of their route schedules.

TIP: In marine traffic terms, "port" is the left side and "starboard" is the right side.

POWERBOATS

As much as I love a warm summer day on the Puget Sound, paddling in an urban area with busy boat traffic can be stressful. Powerboats are usually in a hurry and are unpredictable. More often than not, when I've been in open water and had powerboats coming my way at full speed, no matter how hard I paddle to stay clear they always seem to be going my way. Powerboats under full power can create large wakes behind them. These wakes may go on for miles before dissipating or hitting shore. If you're uncomfortable with rough water, keep an eye out for such waves. If you like to surf, such waves can be quite large and surfable. Just make sure you're not surfing into an incoming boat.

MAKING YOURSELF VISIBLE

Stand up paddlers, when standing on their boards, are far more visible to boaters then kayakers are. Nonetheless, you should find ways to make yourself more visible to boaters. If you're wearing a PFD, find one with silver reflector strips. Consider wearing lighter colors, or even a light colored pair of shorts over your wet suit. Stick silver reflector tape on both sides of your paddle blade. I have white electrical tape stripes on my paddle shaft. If a boat is coming toward you and you're unsure of its path, wave your paddle overhead; reflector strips on your paddle blades will help visibility.

FISHING

Stand up paddleboards make great fishing platforms. Calvin Tom, founder of Boardfisher.com in San Diego, witnessed his friend Mish catching a forty-pound white sea bass from his board. Calvin also catches lobster from his board at night. Calvin started Boardfisher to sell fishing rigs for long boards, but when stand up paddleboards became more common he began to see the advantages. His fishing rigs include a milk carton crate attached to the nose of the board. PVC tubes in the milk crate support fishing poles, while the crate itself stores extra gear.

Calvin recommends having strong stand up paddling skills in order to maintain good board balance while fishing and to avoid finding yourself in weather and water conditions above your skill level. Surfing with a fishing rig is not recommended because a capsized board will dump your gear into the water and may be difficult to flip back over with fishing poles attached. Make sure to check your local fish and wildlife regulations prior to going out.

SAILING

Several SUP manufacturers are now building boards that can accommodate sails, effectively transforming them into windsurfing boards. Other companies have smaller fabric sails that can be stored in a compact form flat on your board. Trying to get somewhere quickly on a standard 12-foot SUP can be slow going in mild wind, yet sailing can really speed up your progress. You might consider using a sail on a long trip or overnight journey when your board is loaded with heavy gear.

Make sure to test the sail in a safe, uncrowded area before taking it out to open water. Until you're fully comfortable with your sail, bring a paddle that can be strapped to your board in case you need assistance getting home.

Paddler Dave Quasha after a session surfing the Washington coast.

CHAPTER 4

Nikki Gregg surfing at Steamer Lane, Santa Cruz, California

SURFING

Learning to surf with a SUP is actually easier than on a surfboard because the large board makes it easier to catch waves, especially smaller waves. Plus you're already standing up and don't have to get to your feet to surf. The longer board is faster, which allows you to catch waves earlier than surfboards, thus getting you more waves and longer rides because the extra flotation will hold you up as the wave power diminishes near the shore.

While a typical surfboard used to be 11–12 feet, experienced surfers are now using boards as short as 6 feet because they offer more control and better performance on steeper waves. However, big wave surfers such as California's Evan Lloyd prefer 11–12 foot boards that allow the speed necessary to catch giants such as Mavericks. The length and speed benefits of a SUP are allowing people to surf areas inland of the coast, where surfing was previously absent. Hours from a coast you may be able to surf freighter waves as a sea kayaker might—except a SUP surfs much better!

Because stand up paddleboards enable a person to catch more waves than traditional surfers, tension has increased in already crowded surf spots. It's important to be respectful of other surfers, and to be a good ambassador of stand up paddling by giving away more waves than you take.

WHERE DO WAVES COME FROM?

Waves are generated by large storms in the ocean, which build swell that eventually reach our coasts. This distance traversed by waves across open water is called fetch. When the swell begins to

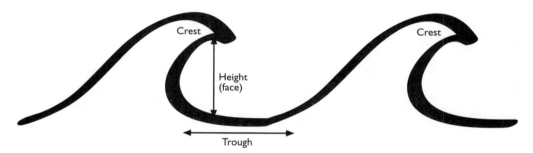

Crest

Crest

Height
(face)

Trough

Profile of waves

touch the ocean bottom, it builds up and with no place to go, falls onto itself, thus creating waves.

TYPES OF WAVES

Experienced surfers prefer certain types of waves for best performance. Some like hollow barrels while others like gentle peeling waves.

Peeling. Great for beginners, a peeling wave is a green wave with a nice shoulder that provides easy surfing. It breaks from one side, gently crumbling over itself. These are my favorite waves.

Dumping or close-outs. These usually occur on steeply angled beaches. Waves approach the beach and break abruptly on the steep beach with nowhere to go. They break crest to crest, creating a noticeable barrel and booming sound. Avoid these.

Peeling wave

Close-out or dumping wave

Tube or barrel wave

Tubes or barrels. Tubes break in shallow water, e.g., at a reef or in low tides. They begin to curl over and break on one side and then eventually close-out. The "green room" is the space created inside the curl of a wave, where surfers may be completely covered by a tube or cylinder of moving water. These waves are for advanced surfers only, because surfing shallow breaks can be quite painful or dangerous during wipeouts.

Crumbling waves. These waves break in multiple locations along the crest and have no interesting form to most surfers. Often created by onshore winds (winds headed toward shore), the tops of these waves get blown over themselves and in some cases flattened. These are okay for beginners but more experienced surfers prefer waves with a more consistent shape.

Crumbling or mushy wave

Wave face

Point break

Beach break

Surfing can be a lot like music: everybody has a personal preference. Some like jazz, some like rock and roll. Likewise, every surfer has a favorite type of break that produces a certain kind of wave.

Point break. When waves hit an extended point of land, they refract around the point, causing a fan effect that many surfers like. Waves may begin to break on the inside of the point in perfect lines that sometimes last for a long time depending on how close the land is on the other side of the point. These tend to be gentle waves, sometimes tubing or peeling depending on the location.

Beach break. Wide open bays or long lengths of beach with sandy bottoms create a beach break. Waves often come into shore breaking unevenly due to the sand shifting below from the wave energy. Wave form can be unpredictable, with peeling waves in one area and crumbling in others. These are great beginner beaches because they tend to have a wide expanse of beach and several choices of waves to surf. Many expert surfers will avoid beach breaks, preferring waves with more consistency.

Reefs. Waves jack up when hitting a reef. Tube or barrel waves are common on reef breaks, but

Reef break (above)

Jetty break (above)

River break (below)

gentle peeling waves can occur as well. Unlike the shifting sand bottoms of beach breaks, reefs create consistent waves throughout the year. Most waves in places like Hawaii or Tahiti are reef breaks.

Jetties and piers. These man-made obstructions create different effects when waves collide with them. In Southern California, surfers are known to surf through narrow pilings at some beaches. Waves either crash into jetties or refract around them, similar to a point break.

River mouths. Outgoing river current colliding with incoming waves can create large powerful waves. Even with very little outgoing current and a small swell, waves of considerable size and shape can jack up when you least expect it. Be aware that the outgoing river current can act like a rip tide and pull you out to sea. (See below.) As with a rip tide, paddle parallel to shore to escape.

RIP TIDES

A rip tide occurs when the water that has come onto the beach escapes via a sand channel back to the sea. They tend to be very strong currents because a great volume of water is compressed into a narrow channel, thus carving the channel even deeper in the sand. They can be very useful for surfers trying to get to waves further out. At some beaches, the rip tide can be found where there are no waves or at a flat section in the middle of a wave. A rip tide might also resemble a section of rough, unsettled water in between waves. On big days, or on crowded beaches, paddlers use the rip tide to paddle back to the line up. It's also an area where no one is surfing, so it's safe to paddle out without worrying about collisions. On big surf days or in storms, rip tides can be hazardous and can pull surfers out to sea. Surfers are sometimes pulled out too far, only to find themselves in waves larger than they were hoping for. If you get caught in a rip tide, paddle hard parallel to the beach to exit the flow of water. Rip tides are also common along rock jetties, which can be hazardous if you're not experienced. A rip tide in a surf zone is different than a tide rip, which will be explained later.

CURRENTS

Many beaches have shore currents that run parallel to the beach, that can push you away from your desired location very quickly. These are called longshore currents. If you're caught in a longshore current, use landmarks to hold your position. Large waves such as Mavericks in California are known for their heavy currents, areas of rough water, and rocks that surfers must paddle through for some distance to get to the break.

WIND

Wind has a strong effect on surf, either making it better or flattening wave faces.

Top View

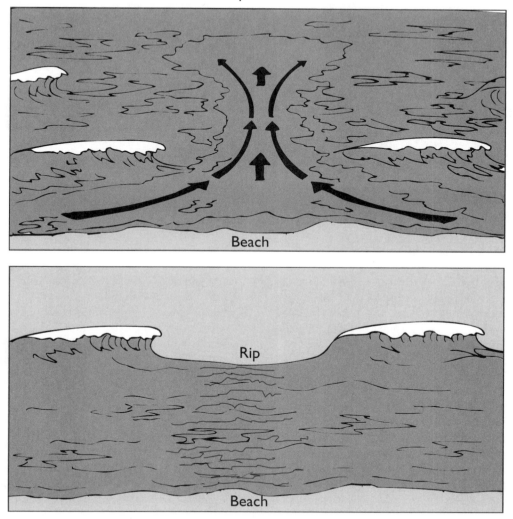

Beach

Rip

Beach

Front View

Surf rip

Wind can also create hazardous conditions. The direction of the wind can also affect your experience on the water.

OFFSHORE WINDS

Wind blowing from the beach toward the waves is called an offshore wind. Offshore winds are preferred by surfers because they keep the wave faces intact for long periods of time, providing longer rides before the wave collapses. Paddling into offshore winds can require extra effort because you're paddling into the wind. In some cases these winds are so strong that you can't catch the wave. Generally up to 10 miles per hour is good for this effect. The south shore of Oahu is known for its consistent daily offshore winds in summer. Sometimes you don't feel the wind until you drop in to a wave and a rush of wind-powered spray sweeps past you. Sometimes it's so strong you can't see. Often you need to catch the wave deeper or closer to where it breaks to even surf it. Offshore winds can be dangerous because they can push you out to sea. In areas where heavy current, big waves, or large wave-battered rocks are further out, you'll want to keep an eye on your location and not drift out.

ONSHORE WINDS

Onshore winds come from the sea toward the beach. Onshore winds push the wave faces down, shortening the wave set period and flattening the waves. Surfers often avoid onshore wind days, but they are great for beginners because beaches will be less crowded. Often wave periods on onshore days will be nine seconds or less, meaning that waves will be closer to each other.

In some cases, wind will blow from the side, giving you both an offshore and onshore effect. Most surfers prefer no wind, or light offshore winds.

HOW TO PREDICT SURF: SURFING FORECASTS

There are several ways to predict the surf at your favorite beach. Thanks to the Internet, surf forecast websites are common. These sites list a lot of important information for several days out or in real time, including wind speed and direction, wave period, swell direction, air pressure, water temperature, tide levels, wind chill, swell size, and air temperature. Many websites also have real-time buoy data for your area. Some sites even show the exact angle at which the swell is arriving, using compass directions as a guide. Here's an example:

```
360 or 0 = N
       45 = NE
       90 = E
      135 = SE
      180 = S
      225 = SW
      270 = W
      315 = NW
```

A standard surf forecast will include the time and date of the forecast and look like this:

Surf Size: 14ft 16secs / Swell Height: 15ft / Swell Direction: 220 degrees / Wind ESE 11 kts / Air Temperature 60F / Sea Temperature 49F.

Popular sites include Magic Seaweed, Surfline, and StormSurf. Each has their pros and cons. I also use NOAA's sites, which have fewer bells and whistles, yet seem to be just as accurate. I use the NOAA site for inland waterway marine forecasts, which are not listed on the other sites. If you have an iPhone or similar handheld device, there are several apps available for checking surf forecasts and current conditions. Some websites use star ratings to judge the quality of the surfing on any given day. These can be misleading, as every break is different; what works in one location will be different in another.

Some websites use marine radio to assist with surf predictions. NOAA broadcasts 24 hours a day on several channels, giving wind speed, air temperature, swell height and period, and any coastal storm warnings. You can buy a handheld marine radio or use a VHF radio. Some cars have a weather band on the radio that broadcasts both marine and inland weather forecasts and storm warnings.

I also like webcams, which give you real time video or still coverage of a specific location so you can determine wind, wave size, or even the size of the crowd prior to leaving home. Watching a certain spot break in different conditions or tide levels to see how the wave changes can be very educational. On some of the better webcams you can watch surfing in action. If the webcam is owned by an individual who does it for fun, you can ask them to direct the camera to a more desirable angle.

In addition to checking the surf forecast websites, it's wise to gather local knowledge of a surf spot, such as where the break is best at high or low tides, and which direction to look for offshore winds. There are also a few websites and books that give detailed information on the preferred conditions of specific beaches. Every beach is different. Some are easy to forecast, others are very difficult. One of my favorite stretches of coastline in the Pacific Northwest contradicts all common knowledge of when waves break best. For most beaches, the longer the period is, the more powerful the waves are. In this location, you want a much shorter period than usual to even get waves to the beach. Several times I've seen surf forecasts for this area that listed up to 18-second periods, and up to 15-foot waves in a favorable direction. Once, the highway that skirts the beaches was filled with surfers. The parking lots were filled, and my cell phone was ringing off the hook from friends excited about the seemingly perfect conditions. But there were no waves, because the period was far too much for the region; thus all swell was passing further offshore and missing every beach.

Despite all the websites, marine radio forecasts, or TV weather forecasts, it's still possible to drive to the beach and find conditions that completely contradict the forecasts. I remember one hot summer weekend day in which the forecasts predicted no surf. The beaches and roads were empty, except for the occasional logging truck. I happened to be at the coast for work reasons and had my board with me.

Stand up paddler Bobby Arzadon surfs the waves.

The great thing about a SUP is that if there's no surf, you can still go for a nice flatwater paddle. But on this day as I approached the beach, I immediately saw whitewater, then swells offshore. Totally stoked, I pulled over at a favorite spot. The parking lot was empty, there was no one in the water, and there were perfect chest-high conditions with a light offshore wind. I surfed for three hours before any other surfers arrived.

Many surfers, who fear overcrowding of their favorite breaks, won't give out information on where to go and when. Some might send you in the wrong direction. I've even seen surf shops give incorrect info or send new customers to the more popular beginners breaks to keep other areas untouched. When I was starting out and didn't know this, I once posted sensitive location info on a chat room, which wasn't well received by a few other surfers. The more you surf, the more you'll figure out which breaks you like best, and how to navigate the nuances of the surfing lifestyle.

TIP: Don't trust a surf or weather forecast longer than a few days out. Especially if a friend tells you the surf will be great seven days out. This is why surfing contests close registration a week prior. If a forecast is poor, competitors will cancel their registrations.

SURFING GEAR FOR THE NOVICE

Much of the gear needed for stand up paddling works in a variety of paddling venues and other water sports. Stand up paddleboard surfing has a few specific gear requirements.

BOARDS

A 10- to 12-foot board, a minimum of 30 inches wide, is recommended. Stability is more important than length. Smaller paddlers can get away with a more narrow board providing they have good stability on flatwater. Make sure your board has a rubber traction pad on the deck. If not, you can apply surfing wax for grip, which comes in bars or a spray can. Some boards don't have enough rubber traction, so wax can fill in where you need it. Fins can be any arrangement when you start out. Over time, you'll find which fin setup works for you and the type of surfing you want to do.

PADDLES

Your paddle should be 8 to 15 inches taller than you. Some paddlers like a shorter paddle for surfing, but I like the extra power and control from a longer paddle. A longer paddle also helps in bracing against large waves or in rough water. Adjustable paddles allow you to try different lengths, or to use a longer length for touring and a shorter length for surfing. Fiberglass paddles are stronger in larger surf.

LEASHES

Use a leash both to prevent your board from hitting others when you fall and to avoid losing the board. Make sure the length of the leash is as long as your board or only slightly shorter. A bungee leash might bounce back at you during a fall and they often get tangled around the fin. Leashes do break, so it's wise to store a backup in your car or at the beach.

HELMETS

Use a surfing or whitewater kayaking helmet to protect your head. I prefer a bright helmet so others can see me coming, and for safety. I also like a full-protection helmet that covers my ears. You can attach small waterproof cameras to the top of your helmet, but it does add a little weight. Make sure the helmet doesn't slide around on your head. Helmets also add thermal protection in cold temperatures.

CLOTHING

If you're surfing in cold water, wear a dry or wet suit, especially if you're a beginner. You will fall in often when you're starting out. Always dress for immersion. I always wear a wet suit when surfing in the Pacific

Northwest because the water is cold all year. I also wear booties to protect my feet from broken glass or sharp rocks on the beaches, and neoprene gloves to keep my fingers from getting numb in the 50-degree water.

If you're in a warm climate, shorts or a bathing suit are fine for surfing. You might consider a nylon rash guard on top to protect your skin not only from abrasions caused by friction with the board but also from the sun's rays. Some rash guards are designed to keep you warm as well. Some surfers wear a neoprene wet suit top to add warmth.

For headwear, some surfers in warmer areas wear a baseball cap or wide brimmed hat. In colder climates, consider a neoprene cap or hood. Hooded neoprene vests are a good option for keeping your head and torso warm without the restrictions of a full wet suit.

> **TIP: Carry a backpack to beaches that require a long walk. Pack extra water, food, and sun block.**

EXTRAS

While surfing I may wear a fanny pack, in which I carry a bottle of water, an energy bar, and a waterproof camera. You can also stow extra gloves or a hood. If I need to carry extra gear but don't want to attach them to my body, I'll secure a fanny pack or dry bag to tie downs on my board or stash them in a safe place on shore. In large surf, make sure you secure your gear tightly to your board.

LIFEJACKETS (PFDS)

Most people don't wear a PFD while surfing and are not required to by the Coast Guard. But PFDs do offer impact protection if you're surfing above shallow, rocky beaches. Some big wave surfers wear minimalist PFDs with no pockets (called impact vests) to protect themselves from a wipeout with a shallow coral reef or from the massive amounts of water that may fall on them. I wear a PFD when surfing inland waterways, where boat wakes create sizeable waves. In these areas the Coast Guard requires PFDs.

EAR PROTECTION

Surfer's ear, also called exostosis, is caused by a high volume of cold wind and water entering the ear over time. Eventually the ear canal begins to constrict, limiting your hearing and causing irritation that may require expensive surgery to remove the bone growth. Surfers wear silicone or plastic ear plugs to prevent this problem. A tight yet comfortable neoprene hood covering the ears can also help reduce or prevent surfer's ear.

LEARNING TO SURF

In coastal areas popular for surfing there are numerous programs that offer SUP surfing lessons. This is the best way to learn to understand waves, to learn the basics of surfing, and to meet new surfing partners. If you're planning a vacation to a tropical place such as Hawaii or the Caribbean, take advantage of the warm water and take

Crowded surf break at Cowells Beach, Santa Cruz, California

a SUP class. If you can't find a SUP class, take a traditional surfing class, which will be similar but without a paddle. The basics are the same in terms of learning waves, how to surf a wave, and learning surfing etiquette and safety.

> **TIP: Learn to paddle a SUP on flatwater before going in the surf. By learning the basics of balance, turning, and control beforehand, your first surfing experience will be easier. You might even find small surf from boats or wind to give you some practice prior to trying the real thing.**

Stand up paddleboards are big, heavy, and difficult to control when you're starting out. Begin on a day when the surf is small, in the 2–4 foot range, which is knee to waist high. Find a surf break that is uncrowded or empty so you will be less likely to collide with or get in the way of other surfers. Avoid areas with swimmers, snorkelers, or children by the shore. Losing control of your board in a crowded beach area could be hazardous to others. Inquire at surf shops about where the best beaches are for beginning stand up paddlers.

Once you've found an empty section of a beach, study the waves for a while to determine their size, and whether they are the type of waves you're comfortable surfing. Peeling or crumbling waves are the easiest to learn on. Reform waves are those that form after the initial wave has broken. These are also great beginner waves because they tend to be smaller and less powerful. Most advanced surfers avoid the reform waves so they're often uncrowded or empty. If the waves are too big or too crowded, find another beach or try another day.

Always watch for and avoid any obstructions in the surf, such as rocks or dock pilings. Some friends of mine once passed a perfect peeling wave on the Washington coast and wondered why no one was on it. They later found out that the beach was on Shoalwater Bay, which has lost hundreds of feet of land from erosion in recent years. The perfect wave flowed over the location of a former housing development that had been swept away, so the beach was actually a concrete foundation with rebar sticking out every few feet.

Visually line up the waves you want to surf with a landmark on shore. Once you paddle to your wave, note your landmark on shore and try to stay lined up with it to prevent drifting away from your spot. Wind

Paddling out over surf

and shore currents can easily push you to a more hazardous area.

Find a safe place to enter the water. Don't enter where waves are crashing against rocks or an in area crowded with children and families. Attach your leash to your ankle on shore and wade out to where you're waist deep. Wait for a break between wave sets, then get on your board and immediately start paddling out.

PADDLING OUT

Avoid paddling out where others are surfing in. If you're uncomfortable with the waves, start out by kneeling or sitting on your board while paddling out. If you feel unstable, take a few strokes to give yourself more stability. Paddling adds stability. An old paddling rule is, "When in doubt, paddle." The easiest way to paddle out is to be patient and wait for a break in the incoming sets. Waves usually come in sets of five to seven. If there's a lull, paddle out quickly. Areas of flat choppy water stretching from beach to break are likely rip tides. You can use them to get out as well, but be careful that the rip tide doesn't take you out too far.

Paddle hard as waves approach you. Increase your power and paddling speed as the wave begins to pass underneath you. For small waves up to knee high, stay in the paddling stance, with both feet faced forward. Keep paddling even after the wave has passed. You might move back on the board a bit to help the nose rise over the incoming waves.

If the wave is waist to chest high, start in paddling stance to gain speed, then as the wave approaches place one foot further back on the board to help the nose rise over the wave, and squat down a bit. Don't stop paddling even after the wave has passed. Bring your rear foot back to the middle of the board until the next wave approaches. This method of standing with feet apart and one foot back is called the surfing stance. Speed is essential in paddling over waves.

If a wave is breaking as it goes under you, whitewater and foam may destabilize you. Keep paddling and bend your knees to create a lower center of gravity. If you stop paddling as a broken wave is passing you, you'll most likely fall off.

Look for a line of whitewater where the wave face has broken. Paddle 10 to 30 feet past the whitewater to wait for your first wave. If there are a bunch of surfers waiting for a wave, this is called the lineup. Avoid the lineup until you can completely control your board in all wave conditions. There's nothing worse than nearly running into a surfer on your first day with your big board, and most likely getting yelled at.

> TIP: Make sure you know what size wave you like and what that translates to in feet. Other surfers you pass on the way to the beach will tell you how large or small the waves are. But when you get there, you'll usually find that one person's "small" is too large for you. I've seen it go both ways. Once, a friend I passed on the road told me there were no waves. Luckily I checked anyway and found that the waves were perfect for me.

The lineup

THE LINEUP

If you do find yourself in a lineup with traditional prone surfers, sit on your board while you're waiting for a wave. Other surfers will feel intimidated by you standing tall over them. Talk to the others in the water, which may break the ice if there's any tension. Some surfers feel that stand up paddlers have no business in any lineup. If the vibe doesn't feel right, move to another wave or break. And again, don't paddle to a lineup unless you can control your board while surfing.

> **TIP: Not ready to stand up and surf yet? A great way to get the feeling for surfing is to surf your stand up board while lying prone on your belly. Store the paddle blade under your chest with the shaft and handle facing toward the nose, or leave the paddle on the beach. Use your hands to paddle on both sides of the board, using a pull and reach technique. Wait for a wave that looks good, and start paddling hard 15–20 feet before the wave reaches you. After a few runs, start to tilt the board by leaning your body to one side or the other. See how this turns the board.**

CATCHING WAVES

While waiting for waves, always look to the horizon. Look for a dark line or rise in the water approaching you. Those are waves. If there is an outer reef or point, watch to see if waves begin to break over it. That's called an indicator. Sometimes there's no activity there, then all of a sudden the indicator is covered in whitewater, which means a wave set is coming. Experience at any given beach will help you determine the size of incoming sets by seeing how they break over the indicator. If you see surfers paddling out beyond the lineup, it may mean a large set is coming in. While waiting for waves, keep your board pointed toward the horizon. Never turn your back on the sea.

The Takeoff

Pick a wave that is knee to waist high. Turn your board toward the shore using a reverse sweep stroke or pivot turn. You should be standing in the middle of the board. Look around to your left and right to make sure no one else is aiming for the same wave. If so, either make contact and ask which way they're going, or wait for the next wave. There will always be another. It's like looking both ways before crossing a busy street. Many collisions and tensions arise from surfers not checking for others prior to taking a wave.

If the wave is clear, paddle hard using the paddling stance (both feet facing the nose), which some refer to as the Hawaiian stance. Use hard, short, quick strokes 10–20 feet before the wave reaches you. As the wave begins to pick you up, switch to the surfing stance, with your feet sideways and just in front of your shoulders. Keep paddling. Your forward foot should be the one that feels most natural. If you're uncomfortable switching to a surfing stance, then a forward stance is fine for smaller waves, just as long as you can control the board.

Chuck Patterson taking off at Steamer Lane, Santa Cruz, California

At a certain point, you'll begin to slide, or surf, into the wave. Keep your knees bent, and get lower if you feel unstable. Keep paddling until you're surfing. For larger waves, start in a squat and farther back on your board. If you're standing erect when a wave comes, it will push the board out from underneath you. Always keep your knees bent and be ready. The lower the better.

Use the tail rudder by placing the paddle behind you in the water on the side of the board you are facing. For better tracking, use your lower arm to push the blade down deeper in the water. To turn, push your blade out and away from the board with your outer hand. If you want to go right, place the paddle in the water on the right side of your board by the tail and push out with the blade. If you want to go left, place the paddle in the water on the left side of the board and push the blade down and out from the board. You can also turn the board by edging, which involves pushing down with your toes to force the rails into the water. It takes time to learn how to dip your rails and use the paddle at the same time. Try to surf a wave using the paddle only to turn. Then surf another wave using just the edging technique. On weaker waves, you'll have to keep paddling to maintain speed. If you feel unstable while surfing, you can also place the flat portion of your blade on the water to brace.

STOPPING THE BOARD

To slow your board, rotate your paddle with both hands and twist your torso to the side so that the back of the paddle lies flat on the water near the tail of the board.

TIP: Always aim for the green part of the wave. When you run out of speed, turn back toward the whitewater or breaking part of the wave to gain momentum.

Push down on the flat paddle face with your outer hand to create drag, thus slowing the board. The further the blade is pushed flat into the water, the more the board will slow down. You might have to squat down to push the blade further in the water. Once the board has slowed enough or stopped, do a reverse sweep stroke on one side, and a forward sweep turn on the other, or a pivot turn to bring the board back toward the incoming waves. Use your paddle blade to brace if you feel unstable. It takes time and practice to be able to surf in, turn around, and paddle back out without falling over.

If you need to stop immediately while surfing to avoid another surfer, jump off your board and try to land flat on your back in the water. Hold on to your paddle as you fall. As you rise to the surface, check your surroundings to make sure you're clear of your board and other surfers.

If another wave arrives before you get on your board, hold on to the leash where it attaches to the board. This is called short leashing. Turn the board upright as soon as possible. Hold onto your paddle at the handle and let the blade flow past you. Dive below the wave while holding onto your paddle and board. The shaft may hit you in the head if you're holding the paddle in the middle when a wave passes.

TIP: Turn the board around or get off it before the fin scrapes the bottom. A fin hitting the bottom will throw you off the board.

WIPING OUT

Wiping out is common when learning to surf a SUP. Paddling in rough water is a test of your balance and skill. It's important to use your leash in order to avoid losing your board or colliding with another surfer. Always hold on to your paddle when you fall. Take a big breath before you fall. Try to fall backward and stay as flat as you can; never dive headfirst. Surf breaks in shallow water, so diving increases the chances of a neck injury. When falling flat, the cushion of the water usually prevents you from touching the bottom. Cover your face with your arm and hold your hand behind your head to prevent the board from hitting you, one of the most common injuries in surfing. The paddle can also hit you. As you break the surface of the water, look around to see where your board and other surfers are. If you're held under or feel disoriented underwater, don't panic. Relax and look around to see where you are, then reach for the surface.

SURF ETIQUETTE

Many older surfers will speak with nostalgia of empty beaches in the hot surfing spots in California prior to the early 1970s. The masses discovered surfing in the late 1960s, crowding beaches and surf breaks, and by the late 1970s fights and vandalism were common as were the occasional violent assaults. Most issues were caused by local surfers protecting their local breaks.

WHEN IN DOUBT, DON'T GO OUT.

- Don't stand between the beach and your board in surf. Waves will push your heavy board into you and cause injuries.
- A great way to get to know the waves is to get in the water without your board. Try body surfing a few waves to get a feeling for the power of the ocean and how waves work. Do this in an area where there are no surfers coming in.
- Stay out of the lineup until you can control your board 100 percent.
- Don't be a wave hog. Stand up paddlers can catch more waves than traditional surfers. If you're taking all the waves you won't make any friends. Let a few waves go to others. Give a wave, make a friend.
- Don't turn your back to the sea. Always keep an eye on the wave sets coming in, whether you're by the beach or waiting for waves.

Poor surf etiquette, Makaha Beach, Hawaii

Sometimes tensions were caused by surfers feeling threatened by larger watercraft such as kayaks. There are many breaks where non-local surfers will be treated with scorn and called derogatory names such as "kook." Sometimes locals will be more tolerant if a newcomer demonstrates surfing acumen.

If you're new to surfing, asking a local surf shop where to go will save you from some of these hassles and embarrassment. It's unfortunate that surfing, which is about working in harmony with nature, has become such a threatening undertaking for newcomers and experienced surfers alike. For years as an experienced surf kayaker, I was often treated rudely simply because my chosen craft was different. I was once asked by a lifeguard to leave a beach in Hawaii because kayaks weren't allowed, despite the fact that there were no signs and many less skilled surfers were colliding with each other all day.

As the popularity of stand up paddleboard surfing increases, tensions are becoming common. It's important for you to understand how to fit in at breaks where you're the only stand up paddler or you are unfamiliar with the area. Here are a few tips:

- Sit down on your board while waiting for waves in a lineup with prone surfers.

Standing tall over others can be awkward and intimidating.

■ Don't take waves from the outside of the lineup. SUPs can catch waves earlier than other surfers. Find your own empty wave if you have to surf from the outside.

■ Give waves to other surfers. You'll catch more waves than them anyway, so sit a few out. Give a wave, make a friend.

■ Avoid other surfers altogether. You can paddle your board longer distances with less effort. Paddle to an uncrowded wave or peak away from the crowd.

■ Avoid waves too big for your skill level. Surfing waves beyond your ability is frustrating to both you and people sharing the break.

SURFING COMPETITIONS

Surfing a SUP takes a lot of practice. Where I live, few paddlers can surf SUPs well, so there are only two small surfing contests each year. But for paddlers in Hawaii or Southern California, surfing competitions for SUPs are common all year long, often with 10- to 30-foot waves. Steep vertical drops and broken boards are the norm in such locations. As the sport matures, surfing SUPs are getting smaller and more maneuverable, allowing for quicker turns, barrel wave rides, and even the occasional aerial.

If you're interested in competing in a surfing contest, check the Resources section of this book and SUP magazines for up-coming events in your area. Competing is a great way to meet other paddlers. Beginners can learn a lot from watching talented SUP surfers.

BOAT WAKE SURFING

If you want to surf but live hundreds of miles from the ocean, don't despair. Surfing boat wakes can be just as fun as dropping in on the real thing. It doesn't require tides and can be done all year. All you need are powerboats, freighters, tugs, tankers, fishing boats, Navy ships—any craft that puts off a large wake. I originally learned to surf boat wakes in a sea kayak. Each type of craft makes a different type of wave, and each wave varies depending on different types of weather, tide and current levels, and location. My favorite waves are the ocean-sized ones made by the large ships in certain locations and specific tide levels. To find the locations where these waves break, look at aerial photos and marine charts of your area and search for beaches with the same characteristics as surf breaks on the coast. Determine where the shipping lanes are and whether waves from ships could reach beaches of interest. Study the beaches to see how waves break there at different tidal levels. Be willing to wait up to an hour or more for a ship to pass only to be left wave-less. To reduce wait times, check websites that track your local marine traffic.

Another favorite of mine are the large green waves created by coastal tugs; these tend to form in deep water far from any beach. Similar to the tug waves are powerboat waves. SUP surfing behind powerboats is common in inland areas. With your paddle, you can catch waves on lakes, large flat rivers, or open bays with small boat traffic.

Make sure that you make eye contact with the driver of the boat for a kind of visual approval. Keep in mind that outboard powerboats are dangerous if you get too close to the exposed propeller. Don't get too close to the stern (back) or sides of any boat. And remember that you never have right-of-way over a powerboat, so approach cautiously. Don't surf in a busy waterway, especially if your skills and balance aren't well developed. You really don't want to fall off your board and have a powerboat bearing down on you at full throttle. If you are friendly and respectful, some boat drivers may even press the throttle to create a bigger wave for you. I've had boaters make several passes to help me out with waves.

CHAPTER 5

RIVER AND TIDAL RAPIDS PADDLING

River paddling can be an exhilarating experience, whether you're running rapids or enjoying the slow current of a serene mountain canyon. In either case, rivers are dynamic locations deserving of respect. You'll need solid knowledge and skills to have a safe and enjoyable experience.

Interest in stand up paddling on rivers has grown quickly over the years, with athletes taking boards off vertical waterfalls, paddling class 4 rapids, or exploring the copper-colored rivers in Utah's canyon country.

I first learned to paddle rivers in a kayak and loved floating through crystal clear water over smooth, colorful rocks, or experiencing the Zen-like feeling of surfing a standing wave. Nowadays I'm more inclined to paddle tidal rapids, which provide river-like conditions in a saltwater environment.

Unlike whitewater kayaking, with a SUP there's no need to learn how to wet exit or Eskimo roll. But there are skills required to safely navigate your way down a river. You should come to rivers with solid flatwater paddling skills, and you should learn in slower rivers before advancing to whitewater. Master the basics and always paddle with someone more experienced. Rivers can be very dangerous places.

If you have river kayaking experience, the only difference is that you'll be standing up and learning how to balance in rough moving water. Many of the strokes used in kayaking rivers are the same as or similar to those of a SUP. Stand up paddleboard and kayak manufacturers are now building boards and gear designed specifically for rivers.

THE INTERNATIONAL SCALE OF RIVER DIFFICULTY:

Class 1 – Easy. Light current with a few riffles and small rapids, and few or no obstructions. Easy self rescue.

Class 2 – Novice. Easy waves, wide open channels, little difficulty, and rocks that can be avoided with some skill. Some scouting from shore.

Class 3 – Intermediate. Rapids that might require complex maneuvering, narrow passages, fast current that requires good board control. Strong eddies, powerful current effects, possible large waves, and strainers. Scouting necessary.

Class 4 – Advanced. Long and violent rapids requiring precise board control and scouting. A quick reliable eddy turn is required to initiate maneuvers. Self rescue is difficult and group assistance for rescue requires practiced skills.

Class 5 – Expert. Extremely difficult with long, narrow, congested and very violent rapids that must be scouted from shore. Rescues and swims are difficult.

Class 6 – Extreme. Nearly impossible and very dangerous. Experts only with all precautions taken. A significant hazard to life.

Each class is often also described with a - or + to show a more specific level description. For example, a class 2 river might have sections of 2+ or 2-indicating slightly more or less difficulty.

Class 1 river

Class 2 river

LEARNING TO PADDLE RIVERS

One of the best ways to learn about paddling rivers is to take a whitewater SUP or kayaking class or to ask an experienced whitewater kayak instructor to give you a one-on-one class with your board. At this time there are only a few instructors who teach SUP river paddling (see Resources). A Swiftwater Rescue Training class is also a wise choice prior to going on the river. If your area has yet to create a SUP paddling club, you may want to join a local kayak club to network with other paddlers and go on club trips.

Never paddle alone, even if you're an experienced paddler. This cannot be stressed enough!

UNDERSTANDING RIVERS

Before you go on any river trip, research which river is best for your skill level. If you're seeking a mellow flatwater

Class 3 river

Class 4 river

experience, a class 1 river is ideal. Class 1 has some current and some small riffles. If you're seeking a whitewater experience and have solid SUP experience, you should start on a class 2 river, which has a variety of light rapids and sections of flat moving water. Also, be aware that one river might have several different skill levels. A river might start at class 1, but become class 5 a few hundred yards downriver. Make sure you confirm this information prior to going out.

When choosing a river, there are online sources such as American Whitewater (www.americanwhitewater.org) that can provide you with river descriptions, current flows, photographs, and river classifications. Research whether there are guidebooks and online sources that are local to your region. Join a local paddling club or network with other paddlers on a local online whitewater kayaking site to find fellow paddlers. Local knowledge and experienced paddle buddies on any river are crucial to having a safe paddling trip. You should also have solid flatwater paddling skills before going on a river. Never paddle alone.

RIVER VOLUME AND FLOW

Once you've found people to paddle with and have chosen a river, check the river flows online to get current data on the river. Cubic feet per second (cfs), the standard way to measure the volume of water in a river, is the measure of water flow equivalent to one cubic foot of water passing a given point for one second.

This measurement is affected by rainfall, dam releases, dry spells, and warm weather that can melt snow upriver. Check the weather to see if there has been any recent rain or a warming that might result in snow melt that would create higher flows than normal. Each river may have several optimal levels depending on the type of experience you want, or your skill level. Lower flows will result in exposed boulders, rocks, and logs, while higher flows will cover those up, giving the river an entirely different personality. It's not uncommon for a class 2 river to become a class 3 if the cfs is above or below a certain level.

Many rivers are rain fed, have spring runoff, or are dam controlled. Some may be spring fed, but still be affected by a few of the above factors as well.

By doing your research, you'll find that you don't want to be on certain rivers when they're too low or too high. Websites will list the minimum and maximum flow for each river. If the cfs level is too low or too high for a specific river, this will determine if you choose another river or go at all.

Check the river description to see when it runs best for your skill level. Rivers that have dams usually have a very consistent flow all year. Some dams have annual releases of water to release pressure or to benefit agricultural interests. Paddlers pay attention to these releases either because the river will be replenished after a dry spell, or because the release increases the level of difficulty.

RIVER SIZE

A small river can get up to 1,000 cfs, medium rivers might be 6,000 cfs, while a large river may reach 100,000 cfs or higher. This info is helpful but variable because seasonal flows change and extreme weather, such as excessive rain or snow melt, can bring a smaller river up to twice its size. Every river is different, and flow can vary depending on not only the width of the river but also how shallow or deep the river is. For example, a narrow, deep river will flow faster than a wide, shallow river.

> TIP: Each paddler reads a river's size differently, depending on her experience and point of view. Don't depend on another paddler's perspective. Research your rivers before going out to confirm current data and whether it's right for you.

GRADIENT

Gradient is a river's descent over a period of distance. It's described in North America in feet per mile (fpm) or meters per kilometer (mpk). The gradient can be determined by dividing the total elevation drop by the total distance. Rapids form when one section of a river is higher than another. If a river's gradient descends gently over an extended area, rapids will be long and even. If the gradient drops quickly, the rapids will be steep and possibly severe. Pools form when a section of river bed is lower than average.

RIVER FEATURES

Eddies. Eddies are calm water sections of the river most often used as rest areas or entrance points. Eddies are formed on the downstream side of a rock or obstruction that deflects the river current, creating a depression in the water that is then filled in by reverse current. Eddy current can flow upstream as fast as the downstream current and some eddies have circular currents that are less suitable for resting. You can also use eddies to paddle upstream, paddling from one to the next in order to gain a preferred position on the river.

An eddy line is the clearly visible line between the eddy and the main current. Crossing an eddy line without making appropriate maneuvers with your board will flip you over and sweep you downstream.

Hole end eddy behind submerged rock on a Class 2 River

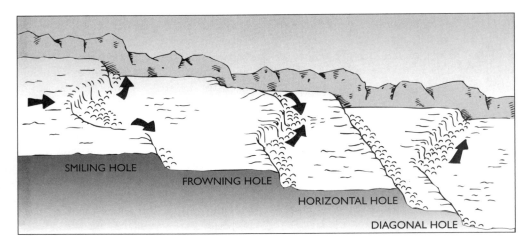

Holes and hydraulics

Paddlers use eddy lines to move between fast-moving current and the eddy. In tidal current areas, eddy lines are not static and can move around if incoming swell or boat wakes affect them. An eddy line above the water surface is called an eddy fence, and requires more skill to cross safely.

Holes or hydraulics. Current passing over submerged obstructions such as rocks creates a hole, or recirculating hydraulic. Often holes are filled with aerated water or whitewater. Holes can be fun places to play, but they can also be dangerous and unpredictable. Deep holes are the most dan-

> TIP: Always scout your run prior to running it. If you can't see around a bend, paddle to an eddy and get out of the boat to scout on foot.

gerous because water is forced to the river bottom and then recycles to the top, over and over again. This recirculation tends to trap or hold buoyant objects or people. Backwash is the recirculating water behind a hole, similar to an eddy. The longer the backwash, the more dangerous a hole tends to be. A "keeper hole" is usually quite large and can hold you and your board for indefinite amounts of time. There are four basic holes to know about.

Smiling holes are the safest holes to run. The middle of the hole is more upstream than its edges, so water pours down and away from the center, thus pushing you and your board away from the hole and back into the main current.

Frowning holes are the worst holes to be caught in, because they can trap and hold you. In a frowning hole, the middle of the hole is the lowest section, thus pushing water from the edges to the center, where a hole is the most "sticky." Avoid these frowns.

Horizontal holes are typically below artificial dams and at the foot of ledges. When the water flows evenly over the top edge of these uniform surfaces, it circulates back into itself along the downstream face of the dam or ledge, trapping anything that falls into it. These are very unfriendly to paddlers.

Diagonal holes lie at an angle to the current, thus allowing water to flow out and away from the hole and back into the current. These are often safe to run.

TIP: If you're caught underwater or find yourself in a difficult situation, stay calm. You'll lose your oxygen sooner if you panic. Think clearly and find a solution to the problem.

Pillows. A pillow occurs when river current runs into and over a submerged obstruction, such as a rock. When you

Dan Gavere portaging a rapid

paddle into one, it deflects you away and downstream around the obstruction, like a force field. Lean into the pillow; if you lean away you'll capsize upstream.

Rooster tails. These occur when river current collides with a rock and creates a spray of water. If the rock faces downstream, the water pushes up and sprays over the rock. If the rock faces upstream, the water is pushed more vertical. Avoid rooster tails.

Tongues or downstream V. These are formed when the main current above a rapid gets squeezed into one centralized flow of water heading downstream. This flow is often smooth and green, and allows easy passage between rapids to a lower pool. Always look for a tongue when you're seeking to move downriver quickly and effortlessly.

Standing waves. These form where the current flows over a rock or ledge, creating a flowing depression that is sometimes deep enough to create whitewater

> TIP: Rocks are your friends. Lean into rocks if you have a close encounter. If you lean away, you'll flip upstream. The same physics apply to ocean waves.

Standing wave

Strainer across river

resembling a peeling or breaking ocean wave. Paddlers surf standing waves much like they do in the ocean, while not moving up or down the river. Rivers such as the Colorado near Glenwood Springs have river-wide standing waves popular among kayakers and stand up paddlers.

Wave trains. A wave train is a series of standing waves. These are fun to surf and to ride downstream like a roller coaster.

RIVER HAZARDS

Rivers are both beautiful and deadly dangerous. Knowing the hazards and how to avoid them can make the difference between enjoyment and tragedy. Pay attention out there!

> **TIP:** Consider park-and-play sessions, in which you paddle in one location rather than doing a longer distance trip. This will allow you to master basic paddling techniques before moving further down the river.

Strainers or logjams. These involve logs or fallen trees that have fallen into the river, creating dangerous and often invisible obstacles for paddlers. One of the most common and deadly hazards, strainers and logjams have trapped and killed scores of paddlers. The best way to avoid them is to scout the river prior to entering, and to portage that section of the river or to determine a route around the jam.

A good friend of mine was once swept into a strainer. His kayak was flipped upside

> **TIP: To find a hole, look downstream below rocks, ledges, or other obstructions. Look for sudden drops in the elevation of the river.**

down and was held there by several tree branches. By not panicking, he was able to think clearly and find a solution. He removed his lifejacket, which was snagged on the branches, and was released from the jam. Many paddlers have not been so fortunate.

Sweepers. Sweepers are overhanging trees, still rooted in the riverbank, that cause both a visual and physical barrier to the paddler.

Paddler below an overhead dam

Lowhead dams and weirs. These artificial structures create some of the most dangerous entrapment risks. Most weirs and dams run the entire width of a river and allow no escape. The backwash is very wide and long, entrapping anything for a significant distance downstream. It is very difficult to escape. Avoid at all costs. In 2010 two experienced SUP paddlers drowned after being swept into a lowhead dam.

Cold water. If you're not properly prepared for the water temperature, you could become hypothermic, which can impair your thinking and judgment. If you feel daffy or absentminded, pull into an eddy or off the river to put on more clothes. Food and water will help bring you back to life.

Always dress for the water temperature, and have extra clothing within reach.

Contrary tides. If you're paddling in a coastal area, check the tide tables to avoid having to paddle against a strong opposing tide. Opposing tides can create rough water and waves.

Wind and fog. Fog can be disorienting if you lose sight of your bearings, and can obscure otherwise obvious obstructions such as strainers, logjams, and dangerous hydraulics. In open coastal areas, wind can make paddling difficult if you are going against it, and it can also build waves if the river current is going against it. Both conditions can make the air colder, so dress properly.

RIVER PADDLING TECHNIQUES

Paddling rivers requires a specific set of skills that can't be learned in any other venue. Choose a tamer river at first to practice these techniques, then gradually advance to more challenging water. **Note:** Never wear a leash around your ankle when river-paddling.

FERRYING

If you want to cross a river without going downstream, you'll use a ferry. Beginning in an eddy, paddle hard toward the top (upstream side) of the eddy, aiming for the upper corner where it meets downriver current. As you near the eddy line, bend your knees, angle your board's nose toward the current at about 70 to 90 degrees, and

Beau Whitehead crossing an eddyline and ferrying across current

TIP: While ferrying, keep your eye on the target destination until you reach it. This will keep your board at the required angle to get you there.

push your downstream rail into the water slightly. This dipping of the rail is called edging. While keeping up your speed and holding your angle, cross the eddy line and enter the current with your paddle on the downstream side. Paddle rapidly while keeping an eye on your target destination.

As you near the eddy on the other side of the river, release your downstream edge and switch to pushing your upstream rail slightly in the water. As you enter the eddy the current of the eddy will push you slightly upriver. You might need to brace, as this maneuver can feel unsettling for the first time. Flatten your board once you're in the eddy.

TIP: Stay Low! The lower you are, the more stable you are.

DAN GAVERE

Considered "the most stoked human on the planet" by Clay Feeter, publisher of *Stand Up Journal,* Dan Gavere is a photographer, snowboard model, professional whitewater kayaker, snowboarder, kiteboarder, and stand up paddler.

A native of Salt Lake City, Dan began paddling canoes at age seven, kayaks by thirteen, and was competing in hundreds of world circuit whitewater kayaking competitions soon thereafter. Named a Paddling Hero by *Canoe & Kayak* magazine, which considers him "one of the most inspirational paddlers alive," Gavere helped put the sport of freestyle kayaking on the map, and is known as the first paddler to truly make kayaking a profession.

While surfing the Oregon coast on a SUP, Dan realized he wanted to pursue stand up paddling competitively. He has since become one of the leaders of stand up paddling on rivers.

Dan offers private and group SUP instruction. See his website for more information (www.supinstruction.com).

Dan Gavere peeling out of an eddy into current

Entering fast current requires a board angle of 70 to 90 degrees, while entering slower current might require a board angle of 20 to 40 degrees. With too much angle, the current will catch the nose and swing the board downstream. Too little angle will stall the board.

PEELING OUT

Peeling out is when you leave the eddy to go downstream. Much as you do while ferrying, get some speed up and paddle hard to the top of the eddy, aiming for the upper corner adjacent to the downstream current. Make sure your paddle is on the downstream side. Before you begin to cross the eddy line, squat to stay low, and angle your board to about 70 to 90 degrees. While still paddling, push your downstream rail into the water slightly, raising your upstream rail out of the water. This is called "mooning the current." The current will swing your board downstream. This pivoting movement might feel unstable, so

> TIP: Practice peeling in and out of eddies ceaselessly. Peel out of an eddy, then back into the same eddy. Repeat again and again. Ferry out of the same eddy to another eddy across or in the middle of the river. Repetitive practice will build expertise. In tidal currents, begin when the current is minimal, and gradually the current will increase. By max ebb, you should be comfortable with ferrying and peeling in and out in faster current.

stay low and prepare to brace if you feel unstable. It is crucial to edge downstream when entering currents; edging upstream will cause instant flipping.

A variation of peeling out involves ferrying out of the eddy to the middle of the river to another eddy, then mooning the current with your paddle on the downstream side, which will swing your nose downstream. This will help you learn better directional control.

PEELING IN

As soon as you begin heading downstream, immediately start paddling back to the eddy you just left. Reenter the eddy by peeling in. Gain speed and cross the eddy line at a steep angle while lowering your upriver rail in order to moon the opposing current in the eddy. Paddle on the upstream side, lean upstream, and stay low! The upstream current in the eddy will swing your nose upriver. Bend your knees and prepare to brace on the upstream side. Some paddlers have a tendency to stop paddling as soon as they reach the eddy line, but the eddy line is an unstable place to be and paddling will help you bridge the thin gap between fast, opposing currents. Often the eddy line will hold you there, making it difficult to make it the rest of the way into the eddy. Paddle hard over the eddy line and don't stop until you're completely in and stable. It's common for beginners to relax too soon and flip. For experienced paddlers, unstable areas such as eddy lines offer excellent play spots that allow vertical maneuvers.

This page and opposite page: *Nikki Gregg going over a steep drop, falling, swimming, and getting back on her board*

EDDY HOPPING

It's possible to paddle upriver by linking eddies on rivers with a slight gradient. While in the safety of an eddy, look above or around you to find upstream eddies. Plot a path. If the eddy of interest is directly upstream, paddle hard to the top edge of your eddy to the corner adjacent to the downstream current. Angle your board toward the eddy line just slightly to enter the current, but don't lower your downstream rail. As soon as you begin to enter the current, straighten the board so it faces upstream. With your paddle on the current side, immediately take fast forward strokes, using a short, fast cadence as you leave the eddy. The key here is to avoid letting the downstream current catch your nose and swing you downstream. Make sure your nose is facing upriver. As soon as you reach the eddy above, ferry over its eddy line by raising the rail on that side. You can also enter an eddy at an extreme angle without having to edge. You might need to stand further back on your board to prevent the nose from digging into the downstream current.

Sometimes, in order to go upstream, you might have to ferry to an eddy in the middle of the river, or across the river, then go upstream. Start out on slow rivers until your skills are developed.

FALLING AND SWIMMING

After you've fallen off your board, get back on as soon as you can. Don't let go of your paddle. If you're without a leash, swim as hard as you can to get to your board. Climb on and if you can't stand up, paddle on your knees until you can reach the safety of an eddy. If you can't reach your board and are being carried by the current downstream, keep your feet up to avoid hitting rocks or getting trapped. Swim as hard as you can to an eddy but don't stand up until you're in less than a foot of water. Even in very shallow water with current, it's possible to have your feet caught between rocks, which can lead to a sprain or entrapment. If you use a leash, you'll be able to retrieve your board more easily.

If you're uncomfortable standing up on the river, paddle on your knees to lower your center of gravity. Keeping your knees as far apart as possible will help. The downside to paddling on your knees is that falling off is more likely and you'll have less control of the board. Don't sit on the board with your feet over the side, as they may strike rocks.

GEAR FOR RIVER PADDLING

River paddling requires equipment specific to the river environment. Although some gear used on rivers has already been highlighted in chapter 1, Getting Your Gear On, there are a few additional items to consider that will make your river trips safer and more enjoyable.

Helmet. Helmets are mandatory for whitewater paddling. I prefer a paddling

helmet with ear protection. A lot of helmets look cool but provide minimal protection and are essentially buckets with a strap that you wear on your head. You never know how you're going to fall, so more is better when it comes to protecting your head.

Look for a helmet that protects your ears, forehead, and the back of your head while still being light and comfortable. Some helmets come with a sun visor, which is useful on bright days. Make sure your helmet fits your head well and doesn't slide around. A helmet strap is essential. You can add or remove helmet foam on the inside

to insure a proper fit. Many river paddlers use the full-face protection models that look like motorcycle helmets.

PFD. A lifejacket (Type 3 PFD) is essential in river paddling. They add extra padding in case of a fall, they add additional warmth in cold water, and they provide storage for important items such as a whistle, knife, and energy bar. In the case of a swim or injury, a PFD will help keep your head above water, especially in turbulent water. Some PFDs come with a quick release tow-belt system that allows you to attach your leash and strap to a tow bag for rescues. If your leash gets snagged in the

Nikki Gregg and Dan Gavere properly equipped for paddling a river

river, you can release it by pulling the quick release lever.

Throw bag. A throw bag is a fabric bag with 40–70 feet of floating nylon rope that is used for throwing to a swimmer or to connect to an attachment point on a board (or a kayak) during a rescue. Throw bags are essential safety items. They can be attached to certain PFDs that have the quick release harness loops around the lower section, or they can be attached to your board. The line doubles as a clothesline at camp, and is useful for hauling boards up cliffs during portages.

Fins. Many river paddling boards come with rubber fins that flex when they hit a rock. Traditional surfboard fins can break or chip. It's possible for your fin box to break loose if you hit a rock hard enough. Experienced river paddlers can paddle finless in situations where the river is either very shallow or quite rocky.

Leash. Some river paddlers use leashes, others don't. It's a personal preference. Those who do, often attach it to their PFD with a quick release strap. Remember, *never wear the leash around your ankle.* When you pull the quick release buckle on the PFD the strap and leash separates from the PFD and slides out. This helps keep the leash from dragging or catching on rocks or wood in the river. If your PFD doesn't have a quick release buckle attachment, attach the leash to a nylon waist belt with a one-inch Fastex buckle. The buckle will break under stress from the leash being caught on an obstruction, and should be easily reached so you can free yourself if necessary. You can also connect the leash to a fanny pack at your waist with an easy-to-release Fastex buckle. You should carry a knife to cut the leash in case the above method doesn't work, or if there are multiple snags.

> **TIP:** *On rivers, don't wear the leash around your ankle.* **A snag by a log or boulder underwater might catch your leash and the strong river current would prevent you from reaching your ankle to release or cut the leash.**

Board. Many manufacturers make river-specific SUPs. Some are plastic, others are of a semi-rigid inflatable construction. These are the best choices for boards on the river because they won't chip or ding if you bump against a rock, which you're bound to do. Paddlers often break boards on rivers, so a plastic or inflatable board is a good idea. Consider purchasing a board with attachment loops or handles to grab onto in case of a swim. Inflatable boards can be deflated and rolled into a small size for storage or travel.

Paddle. One of the advantages of running rivers with a stand up board is that you can use some of the same gear (your paddle for instance) you use on flatwater and in coastal surfing. Make sure you use a fiberglass paddle on the river. Fiberglass is more flexible than carbon, and is less likely to chip on rocks. As with surfing, river paddlers generally prefer a longer paddle to assist with bracing and for more powerful strokes. Adjustable paddles are useful if you're not sure which length is best for varying conditions. Carry a backup paddle in your car in case your main one breaks.

Clothing. Wet suits and dry suits are great options for cold water paddling. Use a bootie with good ankle support to avoid sprains while walking to your put-in or during portages. Some companies make booties with special rubber soles for better traction on slippery rocks. Do not wear tennis shoes or sandals because they provide little traction on the board, don't keep your feet warm, and might snag on a tree branch in the river after a fall. Think about a bootie that will allow you to hike out if you have to, possibly carrying your board over rough terrain.

Gloves. If you paddle in cold water, particularly glacier-fed streams, wear neoprene gloves to keep your hands warm and to protect them from sharp rocks on shore.

> **TIP: Stick bright electrical tape on your paddle shaft to assist in finding it in case you lose it.**

Body armor. Stand up paddlers stand taller than kayakers and thus fall further and harder in the case of an unplanned swim. Some paddlers wear motocross, mountain bike, or roller blade pads to help prevent injuries when they fall. The most common item is shin pads. Some paddlers use spine protectors, which are used for motocross as well. Your PFD also helps protect your chest.

> **TIP: I once saw a kayaker friend duct-taping his toes on the river. He had forgotten his booties and had a few minor cuts from walking barefoot on the shore. Unlike Band-Aids, duct tape is waterproof and will hold together longer while protecting your skin from further injury. Duct tape can also be used to fix boards and paddles in the field.**

Water for hydration. River paddling requires a lot of energy, and you'll get dehydrated in both cold and warmer temperatures. Either put a water bottle in a fanny pack around your waist, or use a hydration system on your PFD. While attaching a bottle to tie-downs on your deck may sound like a good idea, the rope or bungee on your board could get snagged in the river. If you use a fanny pack, make sure there are no loose straps. If you're paddling with kayakers, ask them to carry your extra water bottles or gear that you can't carry in your PFD or on your board.

Towel poncho. These are great for providing privacy while changing your paddling clothes in public places. Many ponchos are hooded and designed to keep you dry and warm while you change back to your street clothes. A standard beach towel is an alternative.

Plastic storage bin. Plastic bins keep your wet paddling gear separate from your dry clothes and help keep your car interior dry.

Duffel or tote bag. Most river trips require a car shuttle to take paddlers back to their starting location. Usually one car is dropped at the end of a run to take paddlers back to their cars upriver. Often, paddlers will leave a duffel with their dry clothes, along with a bottle of water, car keys, and some food in the vehicle at the end. For cold water paddles you may also want to stash a thermos of hot water.

Nose plugs. Nose plugs keep water from flushing your sinuses. While flushing your sinuses might be good if you have a head cold, you probably don't want water dripping from your nose for days after you paddle. Most paddlers wear silicone ear plugs or plastic ear plugs. Kayak and surf shops sell both ear and nose plugs.

First aid kit. Store in a small waterproof container or in ziplock bags in your PFD. Plastic kitchen storage containers serve well as compact waterproof containers.

- Band-Aids
- Neosporin ointment
- Powdered sports drink or electrolyte replacement powder or tablets.
- Mylar emergency blanket
- Aspirin, ibuprofen, and acetaminophen in waterproof container.
- Prescription medications
- Chemical heat packs
- Tweezers
- Small roll of duct tape
- Lighter

> **TIP: Take a CPR or Wilderness First Aid class prior to going on the river.**

On-shore first aid kit. Store a more extensive first aid kit in your car. Include items you can't fit in your PFD, such as Ace bandages, a CPR face shield, SAM splint, liquid soap, etc.

Cell phone. Carry a cell phone in a waterproof container for emergencies. There are several hard plastic waterproof containers available for storage.

> **TIP: Find a foolproof way to hide spare car keys near your car. Many a paddler has misplaced keys while on the river. There are few things worse than coming back to your car at dusk only to realize you can't find your keys. Put a spare key in a waterproof container tucked in a zippered pocket of your wet or dry suit.**

Headlamp. In case you get off the water later than planned, have a headlamp handy. Put it in a waterproof bag or case, or buy a waterproof version. Carry extra batteries.

Maps and charts. The US Geological Service (USGS) has topographic maps available to help you determine the location of a river, e.g., whether it flows through a canyon or through an open plain. It will also show roads and local trails that might help you access the river. Maps are especially useful if you can't find descriptions of the river in local books or online resources. If you're paddling near coastal areas, NOAA may have helpful charts.

TRIP PLANNING

Make sure you do your research, use proper planning, and have solid flatwater skills and a paddle partner before going out on the river.

- Take a whitewater kayaking or SUP class and join a local paddling club that offers regular river trips.
- Determine the level of difficulty for a river. Is it for you?
- Go online to local or national river websites to see if there have been recent changes on the river. For example, have recent floods disrupted trees and created strainers? Is a road out, and are there any recent landslides?
- Determine the river's gradient.
- Check the flow using a cfs gauge.
- Check the weather. Has there been recent rain in the past twenty-four hours or does the forecast call for rain?
- Determine the length of your paddling trip and time on the water.
- Check local river regulations, permit requirements, and parking or access issues.
- Create a float plan. Tell family or friends where you are going and how long you'll be out.
- Check your gear. Do you have water and an energy bar? Your leash and knife? Make a checklist to make sure you don't leave anything at home.
- At the river, remember to scout from shore to check for any obstructions.
- Scout the take-out, make sure you can recognize it from the river. Are there any landmarks?
- Remember to leave an extra key at the take-out car, and one upstream near your car or on you.
- Do a last-minute gear check.

WATER SAFETY HAND SIGNALS

Make sure you and those paddling in your group know how to communicate with each other using river signals. Hearing one another on rivers can be difficult due to the roar of rapids or echoes off canyon walls. Use signals to direct your friends away from danger, to direct them to a safe line downstream, or to communicate while surfing. These signals are also used in coastal paddling.

TIDAL RAPIDS (TIDAL RACE)

In many coastal regions, narrow gaps between points of land during tidal exchanges can create fast moving currents. Depending on the depth, width, and underwater obstructions, the water can be rough with standing waves, whirlpools, boils, and eddy lines.

Skookumchuck, a massive wave on Sechelt Inlet north of Vancouver, BC is very popular with paddlers. The "Skook," as paddlers call it, flows up to 16 knots of current and is often nearly 8 feet tall. It resembles a peeling ocean wave but runs so fast that only expert paddlers can successfully surf

Water safety hand signals

it well. There are several more waves like Skook in British Columbia, the UK, and the USA.

Since coastal tides change direction every six hours (see chapter 3, Flatwater Paddling), tidal rapids in certain locations can have different characteristics depending on the direction of flow. Tidal rapids are also unique to rivers as the current is either increasing or decreasing. As it increases on the flood, water is filling in and covering the shorelines and exposed rocks. As it decreases on the ebb, rocks and shorelines become exposed.

I like a certain surf wave near Deception Pass that is only available on the flood at about a 5-foot tide level. When the tide is too low it's an exposed rock. When it's too high the water flows over it, creating only a slight ripple on the surface.

LEARNING TO PADDLE IN TIDAL RAPIDS

The best way to learn to paddle a tidal rapid is to start out with lower current speeds. Paddle to the area at slack, which is usually a calmer period between the ebb and flood. As the current increases, repeatedly try to ferry between eddies, peel into the current, and peel out of the current into an eddy. As the current increases you'll have more challenges, but you'll progressively feel more comfortable. Keep your body position low when crossing eddy lines and paddling over rapids.

Many tidal rapids are rough only if there are obstructions such as underwater rocks or ledges, or points of rock above water that may create an eddy line, which in turn creates whirlpools. Boils or upwellings occur when current collides with an underwater obstruction. Boils can rise a foot or more above water.

If you find yourself in rough water, bend your knees to stay low, or get in the surfing stance, which will give you more control of the board. Kneeling is also an option. If you approach a boil, treat it like incoming current. Edge to the opposite side of the boil to allow the movement of water to flow under your board. Keep paddling to maintain speed and stability. In some cases you'll have boils coming up on all sides, an eddy line nearby, and swirly current in between each. Every time current comes your way, whether in the form of a boil, eddy line, or other water feature, edge away from the incoming current and keep paddling! You might find yourself edging on both sides every few seconds to stay afloat. Paddle hard toward an eddy or slower water.

EDDY LINES IN TIDAL RAPIDS

Early in the tidal exchange just after slack, you should be able to cross an eddy line without having to edge your rail into the water. Several hours into the tidal exchange, if you don't edge downstream, you'll be flipped by the eddy line. Eddy lines in tidal rapids are often wider and more unpredictable than on a river. Wind, current, boils, whirlpools, and boat wakes can move the eddy line back and forth.

Tom Swetish crossing an eddyline at Deception Pass State Park, Washington

TIP: If you get stuck in a whirlpool, relax! Most whirlpools don't last long. Try to enjoy the ride, and wait until it swirls you in the direction you want to go, then paddle hard to get out. While in a whirlpool, lean to the upper or higher side to stay balanced. Use your paddle to brace if you need to.

TIMING TIDAL RAPIDS

You should only paddle tidal rapids that are regularly paddled by others. Ask at local kayak or surf shops, or check with paddling clubs about which rapids are best. Unless you're an expert paddler, choose a rapid easily accessible by car. Keep in mind that the direction of the current changes during the course of the day, a fact you can use to your advantage in an area of tidal currents if you watch the current tables closely.

You may be able to catch a great ride on the flood tide or an easy float on the ebb. If you mistime it, however, you may have to "buck the tide," meaning paddle against the current.

On one trip, my partner and I timed the current incorrectly. After slow up-current paddling for probably a quarter mile, we realized the rapids were so strong that we'd have to use the eddies to get to the other side. Once across, we tucked into a little bay that allowed us to portage, preventing us from having to go around a rocky headland with strong flood current. There was still a low tide in the bay, exposing several hundred feet of deep mud through which we had to carry our boards to get to the portage. Lessons learned: Make sure you read both the tide table and current table; and allow ample time to reach destinations that require certain tidal currents for safe and easy passage.

Current tables are different than tide charts. Currents affect the horizontal movement of water, whereas tides affect the vertical movement of water. Current tables are only available in areas of heavier current. In wider areas currents may be light, and insufficient to be much help in pushing you to a destination. But in areas where the waterway is narrower, water becomes more constricted and flows faster. A faster current will considerably slow marine traffic moving against it.

When planning a trip in areas of strong current, make sure you have a good marine chart and a tidal current chart that shows the direction of the currents through inlets and around islands at either ebb or flood. Some tidal charts list the minimum and maximum current for daily tidal exchanges. This information will allow you to take advantage of the currents or to avoid them.

Reversing currents occur often around islands.

Many marine charts and boating guides to coastal areas note minimum tide heights required for a boat to pass through shallow inlets or bays. A stand up board allows you to paddle into areas where boats can't go, but you still need to pay attention to your fin depth to avoid hitting rocks.

You can find current and tide tables online and in printed form. I print or copy the online versions and keep a waterproofed copy in my PFD during trips. Some paddlers use grease pencils to mark the daily currents on their boards. Note that tide and current tables are only predictions; wind, ocean swell, and periods of heavy rain can affect current times.

Current tables generally look something like the following example:

2010 -3-17 5:45 AM PDT	-0.00 knots Slack, Ebb begins
2010 -3-17 7:18 AM PDT	Sunrise
2010 -3-17 8:39 AM PDT	-7.38 knots Max Ebb
2010 -3-17 11:48 AM PDT	0.06 Slack, Flood Begins
2010 -3-17 2:48 PM PDT	5.88 knots Max Flood
2010 -3-17 5:39 PM PDT	-0.07 knots Ebb Begins

Notice that slack has very little or no current, but soon thereafter either a flood or ebb begins. Each cycle increases in a six-hour period to maximum speed, then diminishes back to slack. Slack isn't always calm. Sometimes after a big tidal exchange, water will still be moving before the new cycle starts.

If you're not sure of the current's direction, use indicators around you. A buoy will lean in the opposite direction the current is going. Kelp will be pulled in the direction of the current.

> TIP: If you're paddling against the current, consider paddling toward shore to use eddies to go upstream. Even in large open water areas, points of land can create eddies as wide as a bay. Paddling against them is a good workout, but not very efficient if you want to get to a point at a normal paddling rate. Paddling in a straight line to the point isn't the fastest way to get there. Instead paddle close to the shore, which has less current and an eddy that will push you to the point.

CROSSINGS

To cross a large body of water where current is present, you'll use the same techniques to ferry as you do on the river, but you will apply one of two methods depending on which you prefer. With a tactical crossing, you'll choose a point of land on the other side and paddle toward it angling your nose at approximately a 45-degree angle toward the incoming current. It's possible that you will be pushed off course during the crossing. You can either adjust your ferry angle to correct your direction and try to make your original destination, or allow the board to be pushed to another similar location, then make up the difference on the other side.

If you prefer a more precise method, use a mathematical formula to determine your estimated ferry angle. If crossing at right angles, use

$$\text{ferry angle} = \frac{\text{current speed (knots)}}{\text{paddling speed (knots)}} \times 60$$

The problem with such a method is that current speeds can change during a crossing or wind might affect your progress. For more information on navigating large crossings, read *Fundamentals of Kayak Navigation* by David Burch.

RANGES

If you line up two fixed points on land with yourself, that's called a natural range. If the points become out of line with each other that means you're drifting due to current or wind. You can use ranges to determine how the current or wind is affecting your progress. If the furthest point moves to the right, you're being pushed to the right. Some call this method "transits."

USING A COMPASS

You can also use your compass to determine which direction the current is going, or rather, which way it's pushing you. Using either a handheld or marine compass, choose a bearing for the direction you want to go. If it's 270 degrees, you'll paddle in that direction. Watch your heading as you paddle toward the feature ahead of you;

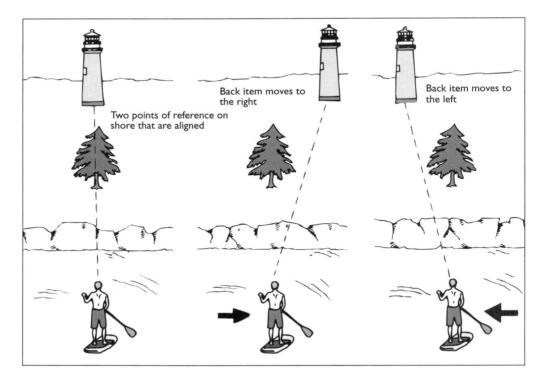

Two points of reference on shore that are aligned

Back item moves to the right

Back item moves to the left

How ranges work

if the heading changes over time, you're being pushed off course. This method works well in fog or during the night when you can't see your final destination.

Another method is dead reckoning, or using a compass course for navigation. Determine your course and distance using a marine chart. Keep in mind that one minute of latitude is 1 nautical mile. For example, if you want to paddle to an island that according to the chart is 3 nautical miles offshore, plot the course by drawing a line from your launch point to the island. Then, using the compass rose (magnetic north) on the chart, and a parallel rule, determine the bearing to the island. You'll have to plot the course ahead of time on land. Let's assume the course is 270 and the cruising speed is 3 knots. This means you should cover the distance (3 nautical miles) in one hour. Assuming little or no wind or current, all you have to do is launch and follow a compass heading of 270 for an hour to reach the island.

Pay attention to ocean swell directions in areas near the coast. Ocean swells can travel considerable distances and collide with an ebb current to form sizeable standing waves. Similarly, wind-opposing tidal current can create waves or large areas of rough water. For some paddlers these effects are a source of stress; other paddlers seek out these same conditions in order to surf or enjoy a rough water ride.

Every December the Deception Pass Dash is held in the pass where paddlers will race the 6-mile course, which starts at slack. The general idea of the race is to paddle as fast as you can on most of the course before the ebb currents get too strong to paddle against. It's one of the few races where you have to eddy hop upstream through thick kelp beds before you round an island and turn downstream with the current. In 2009, seven stand up paddlers were allowed for the first time to compete against nearly sixty-five sea kayakers, outriggers, scullers, paddleboards, and surfskis.

Moving current also occurs offshore and may run parallel to the beach. These are called longshore currents. These can run from less than a knot to 3 knots or more.

> **TIP: Paddling in tidal current may require more open water or ocean paddling gear and experience. If you're in an open water area where you could be pushed out to sea by current or wind, bring along flares and other safety items (see chapter 1, Get Your Gear On).**

TIDE RIPS

Tide rips are areas where current flows over a submerged shoal or shallow area and creates chaotic, rough water. This is also called an upwelling or overfall. Tide rips are also caused by opposing currents colliding, and current colliding with wind. Most tide rips create sizeable standing waves that can move in several directions and can be quite large depending on the strength of the current and wind. Tide rips are not to be confused with rip tides in the surf zone.

Tide rips are a hazard to inexperienced paddlers because of the chaotic wave patterns. Experienced paddlers often play in rips and surf the waves. This type of surfing is different than beach surfing because the wave period is often only 2–3 seconds. In some rips, waves come from all sides. Rips might occur near a tidal rapid where eddy lines are present, making things even more interesting. When underwater currents hit the obstruction, water is sent to the surface, creating the rip. Rips also bring bait fish and organic debris to the surface, which attracts birds and marine mammals such as dolphins, sea lions, and whales.

Rips are a great place to increase your paddling and surfing skills. Use short quick strokes to increase your stability. Just having the paddle in the water makes you more stable. Don't paddle rips unless you're with others. Many rips are located far offshore and may require a long paddle. Watch the weather prior to paddling, as wind or a tidal shift might push you in an unfavorable direction, making for a long paddle home.

CHAPTER 6

RACING

One of the fastest growing areas of stand up paddleboarding is racing. In 2008 there were no SUP races in the Seattle area; in 2009 at least eight races took place, and more than twenty in 2010. In 2009 the first annual 13-mile Round the Rock Race in Seattle had seventy-two participants, while the second annual Battle of the Paddle SUP race in California the same year had 502 participants who competed in several heats. Additionally, SUP manufacturers are producing new race boards every few months to meet the growing demand as the sport rapidly matures.

Many paddlers race competitively while others participate for recreation only. Races have provided a source of networking and community for paddlers, and a new competitive sport for those in regions lacking surf.

Race boards have kayak-style noses that come to a point to slice through the water rather than glide over it. Boards tend to be made out of carbon fiber and are often hollow in order to be as light as possible. Displacement hulls, which are faster than the flat planing hulls, are becoming more common as well. Some boards have rudders or tillers that can be controlled by the paddler's feet to steer the board. Racing paddles tend to be 10 to 17 inches above the paddler's head to provide power and control in turning. Paddle blade widths vary depending on the paddler.

There are currently four categories for board sizes in races. Surfboard SUP Class boards are any boards up to a 12-foot, 1-inch maximum length. Stock Class boards are 12 feet, 6 inches. 14-foot boards have their own class. The Unlimited or Open Class has no size restrictions but is often filled with longer boards, in the 18-foot range. Unlimited can have rudders and multiple-hulls. The Elite Division is for professional paddlers; it has high entry fees and big cash prizes. Board sizes vary in Elite depending on the race.

Race distances range from 2 miles up to 27 miles. The 28-mile Mormaii Molokai Pai'lolo Express Race from Maui to Molokai in Hawaii is a downwind race. In the 2010 race some paddlers experienced surfing 75-yard-long rides from a combination of ocean swell and wind. Races such as the Battle of the Paddle, held in both Hawaii and California, have relays, long distance races, and a course that requires going through surf to start and finish the race. The 6-mile Deception Pass Dash, held in winter in Washington State, requires paddling in strong tidal currents and rapids, often in very rough conditions.

TRAINING

One of the best ways to train for a race is to paddle. On-water training techniques include paddling upwind, using a heavier paddle, paddling long distances or in rough water, and training with others who are faster than you. Off-water training techniques include bicycling, running, circuit and strength training, and swimming. Candice Appleby, a paddler from Hawaii, prefers to cross train by running barefoot in the sand with gallon jugs of sand in each arm and five-pound ankle weights. For core/body-weight training, she swims, paddles her board, and surfs.

An efficient forward stroke is also essential in winning races. Research which stroke is best for you for the type of racing you're doing.

BRANDI BAKSIC

Originally from San Clemente, Brandi Baksic is a firefighter for the city of Torrance, CA. She has been athletic all her life, swimming, running, cycling, surfing, and playing volleyball. She thrives on competition and enjoys participating in triathlons, including national Ironman competitions.

She got hooked on stand up paddling once she felt the thrill of competition on the board and realized it was a fun way to embrace her competitive nature. After racing for only two

years, Brandi, a Luhai Kai and Quickblade team paddler, already has her share of titles. In 2009 she placed first in both the US and International Hennessey's Championships, while in 2010 she placed second in the US and again first in the International Championships. In 2009 she took first place in Oceanside's Queen Surf Monkey competition, which consisted of a 5k run, 1-mile swim, and 7-mile paddle. After finishing third in the Elite Battle race and first in the 10-Mile distance race in the 2009 Rainbow Sandals "Battle of the Paddle" (BOP), in the 2010 BOP she placed second in the Elite race and first in the distance race; she and her SUPCo/LaHui Kai teammates finished first in the relay team race. She placed first in Oceanside's Queen Surf Monkey competition, which consisted of a 5k run, 1-mile swim, and 7-mile paddle. At the second annual Rainbow Sandals "Battle of the Paddle" she came in third in the Elite Battle race and first in the Battle's 10-Mile Distance Race. She placed first at both the First Annual Havasu Paddle to the Channel in Lake Havasu, AZ, and the First Annual Intercoastal SUP CUP competition in Wilmington, NC.

Brandi trains for her competitions by paddling with men who are faster than she is. She believes you need to train hard to race hard, and for longer races you need to train long to race long. Though most of her training is done in the water, she cross-trains by swimming, running, stair climbing, cycling, and weight training.

Starting line of a summer race

> **TIP: If you're doing races that include moving current or surf, learn to paddle and surf on each type of water prior to the race.**

If you're serious about winning, work on your forward stroke so you can move the board efficiently. Research which stroke is best for you for the type of racing you're doing. Paddlers such as Dave Kalama use the Tahitian stroke because the short cadence rate accelerates the board quicker at the start and in swells. Short, repetitious stokes versus long, deep strokes keep the board moving continuously. Watch the nose of your board occasionally when you paddle. With longer strokes the nose may have a jerking movement, whereas with a shorter stroke, the jerking will be smoother, less pronounced. Paddle placement in the water is important as well. You shouldn't be pulling back on the paddle until it's in the water. Your blade should enter the water with little splashing, and exit just the same. If your blade goes past your feet, it will lift water with it as it exits like a shovel, thus slowing you down. Remember to feather your blade when returning it to the catch to reduce wind shear.

Paddler Beau Whitehead believes that many variables beyond your stroke, such as wind, currents, and board length, can affect your speed. In normal conditions Beau can go 4.8 to 5.2 mph on his 12-foot, 6-inch board, but averages 5.5 mph on his 18-foot Bark board. On long distance races he goes a half mph slower in order to maintain a consistent rate of speed for such a long distance. Beau says that for short races of 4 miles or fewer, he paddles between fifty to fifty-five strokes per minute. For longer races, he's closer to forty-five to fifty strokes a minute.

When I rowed crew in high school, our coach used to work with us on our strokes. If you see a rowing shell, watch how the boat appears to nearly stop in the water as the rowers come up to the catch. We worked for weeks to make this jerky movement as minimal as possible. Training techniques include doing the stroke very slowly and being conscious of how the blade enters and exits the water.

At the start of a race it can be easy to tell who will win. During the 13-mile Round the Rock in Seattle, the winning paddlers were using race boards, had adequate hydration methods, and paddled with good posture. I noticed other paddlers whose paddles were too short or too long, and whose backs were paying the price.

> **TIP: Paddle upwind to train. Not only will you get stronger but you also get a downwinder back to your car.**

PRE-RACE PREPARATION AND HYDRATION

Prior to a race, start hydrating the day before a race with electrolyte fluids to avoid cramping. Adding potassium and sodium to your body helps. Don't do any hard or long paddles up to three days prior to a race; do a light paddle the day before the race to stay loose.

Racer Candice Appleby prefers to hydrate the day before by drinking lots of water. On race day, she'll drink one glass of water in the morning, then small sips to keep her mouth moist up to the start of the race. She points out that if your body is properly hydrated before the race, you don't need as much during the race. However, on long distance races such as the 32-mile Molokai Channel, she drank six liters of water in nearly seven hours.

During races Beau Whitehead wears a hydration bladder that he puts in a fanny pack around his waist. A lanyard goes around his neck where the hydration tube is attached. In this way, the drinking tube is only 4 inches from his mouth, so he can drink and paddle at the same time. He carries water only if the race is longer than an hour.

BEAU WHITEHEAD

A City of Bellingham firefighter, husband, and father, Beau Whitehead makes his home in the northern part of Washington State. After racing bicycles for twenty-two years, he started looking for something new.

He had surfed a bit all his life, but was always frustrated by the distance he had to travel to find good surf. Once he discovered SUPs he realized he could get out on the water whenever he wanted. He soon began to compete in and consistently win stand up paddle races in Western Washington.

Beau's first stand up paddleboard was an old windsurfing board he found at a garage sale. He made his first paddle out of an old kayak blade affixed to an aluminum paint roller extender. He is now sponsored by Kialoa Paddles and the Perfect Wave Surf Shop.

In 2009 he competed in and won all the races in the Urban Surf Naish series in Seattle, which led him to San Diego to compete in the national Naish Summer Championships. There he took second place paddling an old, water-logged Isle Surf SUP, competing against racers on elite carbon fiber race boards.

A fitness devotee, Beau has a creative training regime that helps him prepare for races, though fitness is also an important part of his everyday life. To document one of his fire station workouts, he created a fitness video, a popular post to SUP blogs, which shows a variety of ways to improve shoulder, back, core, and grip strength.

You can read more about Beau's SUP life and race resume on his Paddle Surf Northwest Blog: http://paddlesurfnorthwest.blogspot.com.

WANNA GET INTO RACING?

If racing is of interest to you, start training and pick an easy flatwater race, maybe 1–2 miles long. Many paddlers are also entering races for recreational purposes, exercise, and camaraderie rather than for pure competition.

> **TIP: Study how winning paddlers race. What type of stroke are they using? How is their posture? What type of board are they using?**

If you're serious about racing, try other people's boards to see what works best for you. Then buy a racing board, start training, and enter races.

> **TIP: If there are no races in your area, start one. You'll create a paddling community and meet many new friends.**

In areas such as Hawaii or California where stand up paddling has been established for many years, you should be able to find several monthly races to enter or watch. In other areas, the sport is growing so fast that new races are showing up on the calendar all the time. Check for SUP races within other water sports races. In Washington State, Sound Rowers hold many races yearly that include surf ski, sea kayak, SUP, outrigger, and sculling. SUPs are new to the list on many multicraft races, so inquire. You can also find events on the World Paddle Association website (http://worldpaddleassociation.com).

CLOTHING FOR RACING

Flatwater and SUP racing are such good exercise that you'll find that you won't need as much clothing as you would for surfing in cold water. In the Pacific Northwest, neoprene shorts and a T-shirt may be adequate in summer. In colder climates you may want a flexible, triathlon style wet suit, or a 2–3 mm surfing wet suit. I've seen dry suits used for races, as well as layering combinations such as a wet suit top over shorts. Rough, winter races require the use of PFDs and full surfing wetsuits, as falling off your board in tidal rapids or coastal conditions can be dangerous.

Participants in the 2010 Round the Rock Race in Seattle, Washington

CHAPTER 7

SUP FITNESS, INJURY PRVENTION, AND CROSS-TRAINING
by Nikki Gregg

Stand up paddling provides an excellent cardiovascular workout and is a fun way to get exercise at any age or fitness level. It works all of your muscles and can significantly change your overall physique, strengthen your core, and improve balance.

It is important to understand some basic body mechanics involved in a SUP workout to avoid potential injuries and to help improve your overall fitness.

The following pieces by Nikki Gregg, a stand up paddle fitness expert and certified personal trainer, offer tools you can use to prevent wrist and shoulder-related injuries, including stretching and strengthening tips, and will help you learn about your core and why it's important to keep it strong.

RESIST WRIST PAIN AND FATIGUE WHILE STAND UP PADDLING

The wrist may be a small joint, but it can cause some serious discomfort and fatigue after a long paddle if you're not aware of proper wrist angles. What follows is a brief discussion about the structure and function of the wrist, proper paddling technique, and how to strengthen your wrists to protect them from injury.

STRUCTURE AND FUNCTION
The wrist joint is extremely complex, but it is basically the joint where the ulnar and radius bones of the forearm meet up with the carpal bones of the hand. The wrist is designed to be very mobile to give our

Correct wrist position on paddle handle

Incorrect wrist position on paddle handle

hands a full range of motion, with fifteen bones that connect the hand to the forearm. There are also many ligaments, tendons, muscles, nerves, and blood vessels that make up the structure of the wrist. All these components work together to allow us to flex and extend the hand, straighten our fingers, and make a fist.

Unfortunately, the wrist is not meant to support body weight. Too much weight

Correct lower hand position on paddle shaft

Incorrect lower hand position on paddle shaft

coupled with too many repetitions is tough on your wrist joints and can cause tendonitis. That's why paying attention to your wrist angles while stand up paddling is so important.

TECHNIQUE: BE CONSCIOUS OF WRIST ANGLES

Proper wrist angles are essential for avoiding short- and long-term injury to your hands and wrists.

Top Hand

Keep your wrist angle neutral by making sure your wrist does not bend backwards into an extended position. Letting your wrist "break" or collapse along the shaft during your paddle stroke will not only set you up for an overuse injury such as tendonitis, but will also result in less power from each stroke. By maintaining a straight wrist, you can drive down harder with the top hand at the beginning of each stroke,

which will automatically translate into more power into that stroke. Avoid holding the handle too tightly. Relax and loosen up your fingers, even wiggling them around once in a while throughout your paddle session to lessen the fatigue. A tight grip on the handle combined with repetitive wrist movement may result in pain and inflammation, so remember to loosen your grip and to keep your wrist straight.

Bottom Hand

When reaching forward at the beginning of the stroke, grab the shaft of the paddle with your thumb and index finger, but loosely with the other fingers. It will feel like you're making the "okay" symbol. This will keep your wrist in a more neutral position. If you're driving the paddle down with your top hand and rotating your torso properly, your bottom hand will mainly be guiding the paddle through the water and will not be pulling as hard. Applying this method not only allows you to extend the blade further for the catch phase of the stroke, but will also be much easier on your wrists.

THE 411 ON YOUR SHOULDERS: SHOULDER MECHANICS

If you've been stand up paddling long enough, I'm willing to bet that your shoulders have felt sore at least once or twice and maybe even kept you out of the water for a few days. Whether it's a past injury, the wrong size paddle, bad technique, or a combination of all three, eventually you'll be heading to the medicine cabinet (or the liquor cabinet) for some pain relief after a long session. The next few sections provide information about your shoulders to help you keep them healthy, injury free, and out on the water.

The shoulder contains three bones and three separate joints. Many shoulder muscles act as movers and/or stabilizers, and have several functions depending on the shoulder's angle during movement. Of special importance is the rotator cuff, which is made up of four muscles and their tendons originating from the scapula. These tendons help hold the "ball in the socket," are important stabilizers, and help rotate the shoulder.

Injuries to the shoulder occur for many reasons, including acute injuries from sudden trauma such as dislocation, separation, or fracture. However, the most common chronic injuries tend to develop from the following:

1. Prolonged raised position of the shoulders. Holding any muscle in one position too long can cause strain.
2. Repetitive movements and overuse.
3. Doing too much too fast.

Any of these may cause inflammation to the shoulder, which occurs when a muscle or tendon is stressed beyond its limit, causing microscopic tears. Inflammation is actually a normal part of the healing process. However, if the muscle or tendon is not given enough time to heal before it's subjected to the same activity, inflammation can become chronic and cause progressive damage to the tissues.

Activities that require you to repeatedly raise your arms above your shoulders—such as surfing, swimming, and paddling—causes the head of the humerus, or "ball," to rotate up in the shoulder "socket" and narrows the small space between the head of the humerus and the bony projection on the top of the shoulder blade called the acromion process. This causes friction between the rotator cuff tendon and the acromion process, which can develop into irritation and inflammation, better known as rotator cuff tendonitis or tendonosis.

Also, this movement can pinch the subacromial bursa—a sac containing a small amount of lubricating fluid, which lies under the roof of the shoulder—and develop into shoulder bursitis. "Impingement Syndrome" occurs when there is inflammation of the rotator cuff tendons and the bursa that surrounds the tendons.

Another cause of angst for your shoulders is a tear of the rotator cuff. This is more common in people over the age of forty because aging can cause degeneration in the tendons, leaving them more susceptible to tearing. Advanced degeneration may lead to a tear during normal everyday activity. Acute tearing, although less common, can happen from lifting a heavy object above shoulder level, overloading a tendon and causing a tear.

If during or after stand up paddling you experience pain in the top outer part of the shoulder, or pain when lifting your arm above your shoulders (pain that may radiate to the elbow), along with pain while lying on the affected area, you need to address these problems or they will worsen.

STRETCHES FOR SHOULDER AND ROTATOR CUFF

Research studies have shown that people with the lowest flexibility have the greatest chance for injury. Unfortunately, increased shoulder flexibility will not come with doing a few stretches right before an activity, but rather from weeks of engaging in a regular stretching program. Being on a continuous stretching program (not just for shoulders, but the entire body) will help prevent injury and promote efficiency, improve elasticity of muscles, increase range of motion in joints, and minimize muscle soreness.

The following four stretches are to be done after a five- to ten-minute warm up or after a session of stand up paddling. These are not meant to be done with "cold" muscles prior to paddling. It's common for many surfers to walk down to the beach before entering the water, put down their boards, and begin manipulating their bodies into Gumby-like poses without first warming up. This can be dangerous and is not recommended. Going for a ten-minute jog on the beach before paddling may be more beneficial than stretching.

Be sure to warm up for at least five to ten minutes before attempting these stretches. These are static stretches, which means slowly moving the body part into position and holding for a set time. Hold each stretch for about ten to twenty seconds, rest for ten seconds, then repeat. Intensity of each stretch should be on a scale of 1–10. Begin with light stretching (1–3) and increase over time to moderate (4–6) and heavy stretching (7–10). Stretch two to three times per week or more. These stretches are meant for healthy individuals with no history of shoulder instability as they can cause a recurrence of instability. Consult with a physician if in doubt.

One-Arm Shoulder Flexor Stretch

Technique: Standing upright with a slight arch in your back, bring your right arm behind your back and bend your elbow to 90 degrees. Grab your right elbow with your left hand. Pull your right arm across your back and up toward your left shoulder. Repeat on the other side.

Modification: If you can't reach your elbow, grab your wrist instead. Remember to keep your elbow bent at 90 degrees.

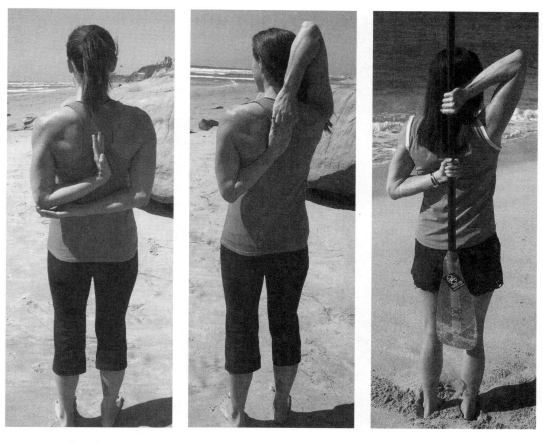

One arm flexor stretch   *Pretzel stretch without paddle*   *Pretzel stretch with paddle*

Muscles stretched: Deltoid, pectorals, neck, rotator cuff.

Pretzel Stretch

Technique: Take this one slowly. Standing upright, raise one arm over and behind your head. Bend your elbow. Bring your other arm behind your back and bend at 90 degrees. Clasp both hands together and hold. Repeat on other side.

Modification: Using a towel or stand up paddle held behind your back by your top hand, move your bottom hand up as high as possible.

Posterior shoulder stretch

Muscles stretched: Rotator cuff, teres major, deltoid, latissimus dorsi, pectorals, triceps.

Posterior Shoulder Stretch

Technique: Stand upright and bring your right arm across the front of your body. With your left hand grab just above your right elbow, and with your left hand pull your right elbow down and around the left side of your body. Repeat on the other side.

Muscles stretched: Shoulder, rotator cuff, upper back, triceps.

Codman's Pendulum

Technique: Hold on to the edge of a sturdy object, bend forward, and bend your knees slightly. Relax your shoulder and let your free arm hang limp. Swing your body back and forth and use the momentum to cause motion at your shoulder. Swing your body so that your arm moves in clockwise and counterclockwise directions. Do not move your arm; let your body initiate the movement.

Muscles stretched: Rotator cuff, trapezius, deltoid, teres major, latissimus dorsi, rhomboids.

PADDLING TECHNIQUE AND EQUIPMENT

Now that you have a better understanding about how your shoulders are put together and how to stretch them, it's time to look into paddling technique and equipment choices that may decrease the potential

Codman's pendulum

for shoulder injury, while improving performance. Also included are a handful of strengthening exercises for the vulnerable rotator cuff and shoulder muscles.

EQUIPMENT

Paddle choice has a large impact on how your shoulders are going to feel. If you have suffered any shoulder pain from paddling or have had a previous shoulder injury that is causing you grief, consider changing your paddle. Look for a paddle that is a little bit shorter, has a more flexible shaft, and a smaller blade size. Why will all this help?

A shorter paddle, one that ensures the top hand does not go higher than eye level when paddling, may prevent the dreaded shoulder impingement syndrome

and muscle strain from repetitive raised shoulder position. Don't go too short, however, because you'll end up bending too much at the waist, possibly causing back strain and also losing your balance more easily. Try a paddle that is about 6 to 7 inches above your head.

A paddle with a more flexible shaft minimizes impact at the catch, meaning it flexes a bit at the beginning of each stroke. This relates to the lower hand, which, while reaching forward to take the stroke, opens your shoulder joint to a vulnerable position. The flexibility in the shaft absorbs some of the initial impact so that it doesn't transfer into ligaments and tendons of the shoulders. Kevin Seid of Everpaddle.com in Haleiwa, Hawaii has developed a Flexi Bamboo stand up paddle with a flexible shaft geared for individuals that have shoulder injuries. The bamboo/carbon hybrid has a smooth, natural feel without the "jerk" at the beginning of the stroke.

Next, a smaller blade with either less surface area or one that features a longer, more slender outline rather than the typical teardrop shape can be a great option for someone with chronic shoulder problems. A paddle with a blade that is too large may cause muscles to fatigue quickly, which will compromise your form, thus causing you to compensate with the incorrect muscles. This may open the door to more shoulder woes. With a smaller blade or longer and more slender-tipped blade, you can vary the power of your stroke more, eliminating some of the "bite" that may be experienced with a larger teardrop-shaped paddle, reducing bottom hand shoulder fatigue.

TECHNIQUE

Make sure to examine technique closely. If possible, have someone take video of your stroke to see how you can modify it. Using your entire body when paddling will take a significant amount of pressure off your shoulders, as well as help you develop a more efficient stroke. It's important to push down hard with the top hand as the bottom hand simultaneously guides the paddle back, making sure you implement a strong core rotation with each stroke. Keep your knees bent as the stroke

is initiated, then as the paddle is pulled back toward your body, bring your hips forward with a little thrust off the board with your legs. For some individuals, paddling with only part of the blade submerged and using shorter, faster strokes works well. Faster, higher rep strokes work if you opt for a smaller blade size.

STRENGTHENING EXERCISES

If you don't keep your rotator cuff happy, then your paddling sessions won't be very much fun. Here are three strengthening exercises that cover all four muscles of the rotator cuff to help keep your shoulder stoked. Check with a physician before beginning any exercise program. Each exercise should be done with more repetitions and very little weight. A resistance band has been chosen for these exercises, but a very lightweight dumbbell may be used instead.

Shoulder Abduction

This exercise is initiated by the supraspinatus muscle, located at the top of the shoulder joint. Its purpose is to help stabilize the shoulder joint and initiate raising the upper arm and moving it away from the body.

1. Attach resistance band to a stationary object at the level of your waist.
2. Hold arm down by your side with your palm facing the attachment point.
3. Grab the resistance band and, keeping the elbow straight, exhale

Shoulder abduction

and lift the band out to the side away from the attachment point.

4. Lift the band to about shoulder level and keep your palm facing down.

5. Do not lift the band above your shoulder level.

6. Hold for a few seconds without shrugging your shoulder and then slowly lower back down to the starting position.

7. Perform one to three sets of ten to fifteen repetitions and repeat on the other side.

External rotation

External Rotation

This exercise calls upon the teres minor and infraspinatus muscles that externally rotate the shoulder. They are found in the back of the shoulder joint.

1. Attach resistance band to a stationary object.
2. Stand with your right side to the attachment point.
3. Hold resistance band with your left hand and keep your wrist straight.
4. Begin with your left hand against your stomach in front of your body with your elbow bent at 90 degrees.
5. Keep your elbow against your side as you slowly stretch the band by moving your arm outward until the back of your hand is facing backward.
6. Perform one to three sets of ten to fifteen repetitions and repeat exercise on other side.

Internal rotation

Internal Rotation

This exercise uses the subscapularis muscle of the rotator cuff. The subscapularis is at the front of the shoulder and internally rotates the shoulder joint.

1. Attach resistance band to a stationary object.
2. Stand with your right side to the attachment point.
3. Hold resistance band with your right hand.
4. Start with your right hand pointing to the attachment point with your elbow bent at 90 degrees.
5. Slowly stretch the band by moving your arm inward toward your stomach, with your elbow bent. Keep your elbow at your side.
6. Perform one to three sets of ten repetitions. Repeat the exercise on the other side.

You'll appreciate a strong core when paddling on rugged coasts.

YOUR CORE...WHAT IS IT?

Obviously by now you know that stand up paddling is an amazing full body workout, especially for your core. But, do you know exactly what your "core" is, what it does, and the many reasons you need it to be strong?

Your core, or power center, is what initiates and supports most movements you make and the amount of force and speed you generate. It is made up of many muscles that run along the trunk and torso that, when contracted, assist in stabilizing the spine, pelvis, and shoulder girdle. The main goal of the core is to sustain a solid foundation and transfer energy from the center of your body to your limbs.

You are only as strong as your weakest link, and unfortunately, for most people it is their core. Do you or others you know suffer from low back pain, hip, or groin strains? Most likely it is because of a weak core. Strong arms and legs without a properly strengthened torso are an injury waiting to happen. Strength must be built from the core first.

With that said, exactly what is your core composed of? It's not only the superficial "six pack" muscles that you see, or wish to see, in the mirror. There are many more muscles involved than you think. Let's take a brief look at some of the main muscles:

- *Rectus Abdominis:* extends the length of the front of your abdomen (the six pack muscle)
- *Erector Spinae:* group of three muscles that run along your neck and back

- *External Obliques:* located on the side and front of your abdomen
- *Internal Obliques:* located under the external obliques and running diagonally in the opposite direction to them
- *Transverse Abdominis:* deepest muscle of the abdominal muscles, wraps around your spine for stability and protection
- *Hip Flexors:* group of muscles located in front of the pelvis and upper thigh
- *Gluteus medius and minimus:* located at the side of your hip
- *Gluteus maximus, Hamstring group, piriformis:* located at the back of the hip and upper thigh (your butt)
- *Hip Adductors:* inner thigh muscles
- *Multifidus*: a deep muscle of the back that helps extend and rotate the spine

As you can see there are a lot more muscles involved in your core than you may have originally thought. So, now that you have the basic knowledge of what your core is and why it needs to be strong, what specific steps can you take to strengthen it? The following suggestions will build your foundation and help you remain injury free, while improving your posture and balance while stand up paddling.

EFFECTIVE CORE WORKOUT— NO GYM NECESSARY

Here are three exercises that, if done in succession without a break between them, will get all your muscles firing in your torso and, over time, make you a stronger and more efficient stand up paddler. These exercises build endurance and strength in

Plank

your back, abs, and stabilizer muscles.

Take a five- to ten-minute warm-up prior to this workout. My favorite is jumping rope or a slow jog. These exercises require a great piece of equipment: your body! You also want to find a weight of at least ten pounds that you can move around fairly easily. I use a rock I found on the beach, or you can use a medicine ball, kettle bell, or a bag of sand.

Perform three to five sets of each exercise in a circuit-style workout. Go from one exercise right to the next. A one-minute break is allowed between circuits. These exercises are for healthy individuals with no apparent health risks or injuries. Check with your doctor before starting this or any workout routine.

Plank
1. Lie down on your stomach and rest on your toes and elbows.
2. Rotate your palms so they face each other and make a fist.
3. Lift your hips off the ground so that your shoulders, hips, and knees are in alignment.
4. Hold this isometric position for thirty to sixty seconds, making sure your hips do not rise or sink down,

Plank to push-up

but remain in alignment with your flat back.

5. Immediately move on to the next exercise.

Diagonal Wood Chop

1. Grab your ten-pound object.
2. Stand with your feet slightly wider than shoulder width.
3. Put your arms up to one side of your head, holding your weight. If you prefer to use no weight in the beginning just clasp your hands together.
4. Squat down and "chop" diagonally across your body to the outside of the opposite knee. Your elbow should maintain a 10-degree bend through the range of motion.
5. Stand and swing the weight back up across your body to starting position.
6. Keep your back flat. Do not round your back.
7. Repeat fifteen to twenty times on each side, moving with more speed and adding more weight as you progress and get stronger.

Knee to elbow

Plank to Push-Up

1. Start in push-up position with your wrists directly under your shoulders. Keep your shoulders, hips, and knees aligned. Keep your head in a neutral position, looking at the ground.
2. Drop down to plank position one arm at a time, then push yourself back up to push-up position one arm at a time. That is one rep. Repeat for ten to twelve reps.
3. Continue immediately to next exercise without rest.

Knee to Elbow

1. Remaining in push-up position, bring your knee in and touch your elbow (or get as close as you can).
2. Alternate sides for a total of sixteen to twenty reps.
3. For added difficulty, bring your knee to your opposite side elbow (e.g., left knee to right elbow).
4. Ouch! Your core should be on fire right now! Take a one minute break and do the whole circuit again.

NIKKI GREGG

Originally from Ohio, champion SUP racer and fitness expert, Nikki Gregg, owner of NRG Lifestyle Fitness Training, travels worldwide and has lived in Colorado, Nevada, Hawaii, and California, all in pursuit of her passion for outdoor activities: snowboarding, whitewater kayaking, mountain biking, adventure racing, wakeboarding, and backpacking.

After discovering stand up paddling, her favorite outdoor sport, Nikki realized it gave her the best overall workout. "Stand up paddling has done far more to improve my physique than any gym work I've done. Plus, it happens to be fun."

Her enthusiasm for the sport, combined with more than ten years of fitness expertise, led her to create a unique fitness program, Stand Up Paddle Boot Camps, which combines stand up paddling with other active outdoor workouts.

Nikki won the 2009 Battle of the Paddle in the Women's Open Class and is a team paddler for both Werner Paddles and Starboard SUP. Nikki offers a variety of fitness training services. You can find out more on her website: www.nikkigregg.com.

Warning: Strength training may lead to doing handstands on the water.

CROSS-TRAINING

Are you looking for different ways to spice up your stand up paddle workout? By transforming your SUP session into a multisport workout—cross-training—you will condition different muscle groups, reduce any boredom that may set in, and reduce the risk of overuse injury.

SWIMMING

Bring your goggles or snorkel mask and wear a surf leash for your next stand up paddle workout. When you're about halfway through your session put on your goggles, place your paddle lengthwise onto your board, jump in, and start swimming. Make sure your leash is attached to your ankle and let your board drag behind you as you swim. Change up a freestyle stroke with the breast stroke every five minutes. There will be a slight pull on your leg from the surf leash.

BEACH/LAND SPRINT TRAINING

During your paddle workout, park your board on the beach and start running. Mix up a series of sprints with a slower pace added in for recovery. Think of a scale between one and ten, with one being your easiest effort and ten your hardest. Begin with thirty seconds of sprinting at an effort of eight and recover for one minute at a five. Over time, increase the time of your hard effort and decrease your recovery time. Repeat the sprints several times during your workout for a set amount of time. Fast-paced walking mixed with slower-paced walking is also an option for those who are not runners.

UNDERWATER ROCK RUNNING

One benefit to living in Hawaii is the option of swimming down to the ocean floor, grabbing a rock, and running along the sandy bottom as long as you can before your lungs begin to burn. This is an amazing way to expand your lung capacity, a form of hypoxic training. Add several sets of underwater rock running to your paddle workout. Be careful with this one, though, because there have been cases of people blacking out from this exercise even while running in shallow water. Be sure to have a partner with you, take turns, and use caution.

It is important to add a warm up, cool down, and stretching to each of your paddle workouts. Be sure to stay hydrated by drinking plenty of high-quality water. Be safe out there and check with a physician before beginning any new exercise program.

Afterword

All around the world, serious stand up paddlers are racing, surfing, running rivers and waterfalls, fishing, completing long distance races and expeditions, and tackling rough outer coast conditions. Other more recreational paddlers are finding that with only one board they can do all of the above or simply enjoy a quiet summer evening on a lake.

It's the stoke and passion to be on the water that makes stand up paddling what it is. People are finding that they don't need waves to paddle a SUP, and from Oklahoma and Ohio to Oslo and Osaka, people are taking to the sport with a passion. Inspired by the great surfers past and present, many paddlers are finding a new home on the water, whether it be a slow-moving river, a wild outer coast, or an urban lake. A paddle, board, and leash are the only gear required, and stand up paddling is an activity that all

the members of a family can enjoy together. On hot summer days I've seen several children on one board, using the SUP like a raft from a Huck Finn adventure. Paddlers new to the sport may have backgrounds such as surfing, wind surfing, kayaking, canoeing, and kite boarding, while others have no water sports experience at all. Surfers in their 50s and 60s are taking up stand up paddling because it requires less flexibility and helps them gain strength and endurance. One of the pioneers of the sport, John Zapotocky, one of the original Waikiki Beachboys, still paddles his board at his home break, at the age of 91.

Stand up paddling has helped me to lose considerable weight, and has improved my balance and stance. The core workout that stand up paddling provides has strengthened my legs, core, and upper body, and it's been a lot more fun than going to the gym.

The magical feeling of moving over water

What are you waiting for? Get out there!

I have also met many new friends and paddling partners.

The intent of this book is to provide a foundation of effective paddling techniques, an understanding and better awareness of personal risk assessment, and a view into the health benefits of the sport. While stand up paddling is in some ways easier than kayaking, practice and water time is required to become competent. My hope is to provide readers with a solid introduction to the sport that allows them to be safe, to visit beautiful and remote places that enhance their lives, and to be inspired by the wonderful feeling of moving over the magic that is water.

GLOSSARY

acromion process: Outer end of the shoulder blade that extends over the shoulder joint, attaching to the collarbone.

bank: River shore or sandbar in saltwater environments.

bar: Shallow part of river channel, with sand, gravel or small rocks.

beach break: Where waves break on a sandy bottomed beach. Usually sandy beaches are flat so the waves are scattered with little consistent form.

beam seas: Waves created by wind that comes in from the side.

beam wind: A wind blowing against a watercraft from a side direction.

Beaufort Scale: Measure for describing wind speed based mainly on observed sea conditions, created in 1806 by Sir Francis Beaufort, an Irish-born British admiral and hydrographer.

Bimini cap: Baseball cap with fabric covering the neck for sun protection.

bivy sack: Short for "bivouac sack," a lightweight, waterproof shelter that is an alternative to a tent.

blade: Wide, flat part of a paddle used to propel the board through the water.

blown-out: When strong onshore winds flatten waves, making it undesirable to surf.

body armor: Usually motorcross pads or the like used to protect the paddler's body in river or big wave surfing.

boils: When water is pushed to the surface, creating a boiling effect that can upset paddlers.

bony: Shallow, rocky river rapids.

booties: Neoprene shoes used for water sports.

boulder garden: River rapids with many boulders.

bow: Front of watercraft.

bow-angle method: Method used in conjunction with a paddle to determine whether a paddler is on a collision course with an oncoming boat.

brace: Paddle movement that assists the paddler in staying upright.

breaking wave: A standing wave that falls upstream on a river; or, in the ocean, when a wave becomes too large for its own weight and begins to crumble or spill over itself.

breakwater: A barrier that helps diminish the force of incoming waves, usually found in coastal areas to protect a harbor or shore.

bucking the tide: Paddling against the current.

carabiner: Metal clip used for attaching gear to PFDs or boards, or for use in river rescues.

carbon fiber: A very thin graphite fiber fabric used to build ultralight boards and kayaks.

catch: Starting position for a paddle stroke.

CFS: The measure of water flow equivalent to one cubic foot of water passing a given point for one second. It is used to measure the river flow levels in a river.

chute: A narrow and constricted portion of a river.

clean: River route free of obstructions.

CMS: Cubic meters per second. Used to measure the river flow levels in a river.

CNC cutting machine: A precise machine run by a computer to cut foam or wood to make surfboards and kayaks.

confluence: Point where two rivers intersect.

contrary tide: Strong opposing tide that can also create rough water and waves.

core: Power center of your body, made up of muscles that run along the trunk and torso, that initiates and supports most movements you make and the amount of force and speed you generate.

crest: Ridge or top of a wave.

cross bow paddling: A forward stroke or turning technique that allows a paddler to paddle on both sides of the board without switching hands.

crumbling wave: Waves that break gently over themselves.

current: Moving water.

currents table: Shows hourly changes in current speeds and directions.

cutback: When a surfer performs tight turns on a wave.

dead reckoning: Determining your position based on a previously determined position.

deck: Topside of board.

deck bag: A waterproof bag that can be attached to your board deck.

deltoid muscle: Muscle that forms the rounded contour of the shoulder.

dihedral: A paddle blade with a spooned or cupped face to grab more water.

ding: A puncture or other exterior damage on a fiberglass surfboard.

displacement hull: A round-hulled board. Most often used for stability or for speed.

downstream: The direction the river flows.

downwinder: Paddling downwind long distances on big wind days, in which fetch creates large surfable waves.

drift: Movement due to the force of wind and currents.

drop: Sudden change in level of river bottom.

dropping in: Catching a wave.

dry bag: Waterproof bag, available in various sizes, designed to keep contents dry.

dry suit: Waterproof suit designed to keep paddlers dry by enclosing them in an impermeable layer of fabric, under which insulating layers of clothing are worn.

dufek: A static side-draw of the paddle that allows you to turn a moving board without taking a stroke. (Originated in whitewater kayaking.)

ebb: Outgoing tide.

eddy: A current of water moving in a direction that is different from the main current, which generally involves a circular motion, and is often found downstream of an obstacle.

eddy line: The interface between the eddy current and the main current, or the interface between a primary downstream current and a secondary upstream current.

edging: Pushing one side or rail of the board into the water to assist in turning, going straight, or in crossing an eddy line.

egg rails: Round-shaped rails or sides of the board.

electrolyte replacement drink: A powder added to water or fluid used to prevent dehydration.

epic: A surfer's term to describe something that is exciting, fantastic, or unbelievably good.

epoxy: A thermosetting polymer formed from the reaction of a polyamine "hardener" that is used as an adhesive or to attach fiberglass to foam in building surfboards. Also known as polyepoxide.

erector spinae: The group of three muscles that run along the neck and back; part of the core.

external obliques: Part of the core located on the sides and front of the abdomen.

EZ plugs: A product used to attach gear to a board using plastic loops glued to the deck.

face: The wall of a wave.

Farmer Jane/John: Sleeveless neoprene wet suit that covers the body and legs.

Fastex buckle: A quick-release buckle that can be used on a waist belt that attaches to a leash on a board.

Feather: To rotate the paddle shaft so that the blade is parallel to the rails while returning to the catch after finishing a stroke. Feathering the paddle decreases resistance when paddling into the wind.

ferry: Using moving current to move a board horizontally across river or channel.

fetch: Effect of wind that has blown over a long distance of water that in turn builds large waves.

fiberglass: A fabric used to build surfboards and paddles.

fin: Fins attach to the bottom tail of the board to assist with keeping the board straight and balanced.

flat: How water is described when there is no surf.

float plan: A plan that that includes a description of your board or watercraft, the safety equipment you are carrying, where you expect to be, and when you expect to be there and to return; it is shared with a responsible party before you leave on a trip.

flood: Incoming tide or current. Opposite of an ebb tide or current.

foam: The frothy whitewater part of a breaking wave. Also the material used to build the form for stand up paddleboards.

foil: The thickness of a board from tail to nose.

following seas: Condition created when wind pushes from behind. The condition used for a downwinder paddle.

FUD: Feminine urinary directional device.

garage sale: Term used for a set-up in a situation in which gear (PFD, board, paddle) is pieced together or borrowed from different people.

gradient: A river's descent over a period of distance.

gun: A surfboard specifically designed to catch and ride large waves.

Hawaiian stance: A term describing the stance on a SUP when both feet face toward the nose.

helmet: Used to protect the head from collisions with others or your own gear, and to keep your head warmer in colder climates.

hip adductors: Inner thigh muscles that make up part of the core.

hip flexors: Group of muscles located in front of the pelvis and upper thigh that make up part of the core.

hole: Where water recirculates behind a boulder or rock that obstructs river current. Also called a *hydraulic.*

hull: The body of the board (or other water craft). It provides the buoyancy that keeps the watercraft from sinking.

humerus: Upper arm bone.

hydration bladder: A container that holds drinking water and can be attached to a PFD, fanny pack, or backpack.

hydraulic: Where water recirculates behind a boulder or rock that obstructs river current. Also called a *hole.*

hyperthermia: An abnormally high body temperature, usually resulting from exposure to warm water warm temperatures.

hypothermia: An abnormally low body temperature, often caused by prolonged exposure to cold water: occurs when the core body temperature drops below 35°C (95°F).

impact vest: A PFD with a foam core that protects the body in case of a fall on rocks, reef, or in large waves.

impingement syndrome: A condition that occurs when there is inflammation of the rotator cuff tendons and the bursa that surrounds the tendons.

infraspinatus muscle: One of the muscles that externally rotates the shoulder, found in the back of the shoulder joint.

internal oblique: Part of the core under the external obliques; the internal oblique runs diagonally in the opposite direction of the external oblique.

international scale of river difficulty: A standard measurement to describe levels of difficulty in rivers.

jetty: Structure that projects into a body of water to influence the current or tide, or to protect a harbor or shoreline from storms or erosion.

J-stroke: Forward stroke that helps keep the board straight.

knife-edged bow: A kayak-style nose of a board that has a sharp center point, often raised above the rest of the board.

knots: A unit of speed equal to one nautical mile per hour, exactly 1.852 km/h and approximately 1.151 mph.

kooks: A pejorative term used to describe beginners or less skilled surfers.

latissimus dorsi: Back muscle that draws the upper arm downward and backward and rotates it inward.

leash: A plastic line connecting the paddler to the board.

leash plug: A plastic plug inserted into the decking at the tail of a board that has a metal bar for attaching the leash.

LED light: Tiny light emitting diodes that don't have a filament that will burn out, don't get especially hot, and are good for night paddling.

lee of the wind: An area of water protected by the wind, usually caused by a large land mass.

lineup: Where surfers catch waves. Look for a string of surfers in a straight line.

lip: Crest of a wave.

longshore currents: Ocean currents that run parallel to the shore.

marine chart: A chart or map used to assist boaters in navigation.

mooning the current: A technique used for crossing eddy lines in fast moving current that involves edging the board with the bottom of the board facing the incoming current.

multifidus: A deep muscle of the back that helps extend and rotate the spine. Part of the core.

mylar blanket: A blanket used in emergencies, possibly after prolonged exposure in cold water or weather.

National Oceanic and Atmospheric Administration (NOAA): A federal agency focused on the condition of the oceans and the atmosphere.

northerly: Winds from the north.

nose: Front end of board.

nose rudder: Using the paddle to turn the board while it is moving by placing the paddle at the front of the board.

offshore wind: Winds that blow from the beach out to the sea.

O'Neill Assault Vest: A compact PFD or lifejacket intended to float and protect the paddler or surfer from collisions without being bulky.

onshore wind: Winds that blow to shore from sea.

outrigger: A canoe with a extension on one side attached to a stability bar that makes the canoe more stable.

overhead: A term used to describe surf that is larger than an average-size person.

paddleboarding: A sport in which you lie prone on a paddleboard and paddle with your hands without using a paddle.

paddle shaft: The long section of a paddle.

paddling jacket: A windproof and waterproof jacket with latex wrist and neck seals to keep water out.

pectoral muscles: Muscle that covers your rib cage.

peeling out: A technique allowing the paddler to leave an eddy.

peeling wave: A wave whose crest breaks gently over the wave facing, often rolling down the wave.

PFD: Personal flotation device, life jacket.

pillow: Current pushing up toward the surface after colliding with a rock. Also called a cushion.

planing hull: A hull designed to lift partially from the water's surface at high speeds.

point break: When waves are refracted around a point and create a fan-shaped surf break, breaking clean from the inside.

port: Left side of a watercraft, when facing the front, or bow. Also port side.

portage: To carry a board, or boat, around a rapid or across a narrow portion of land from one body of water to another. Often used to avoid a dangerous waterfall or hydraulic.

prone paddle: Paddling on your chest.

put-in: Place where you begin a trip.

quartering seas: Wind-driven waves that come at an angle toward your board.

rack: A pair of metal bars on top of a car used to carry your boards.

rail: Edge or side of board.

rapid: Where a river elevation drops, thus creating a rush of water or waves.

rash guard: Article of clothing used for protection against sun and rash.

recirculating hydraulics: Where water pours over an obstruction and recirculates back upstream.

rectus abdominis: Part of the core that extends the length of the front of the abdomen (the "six pack" muscle).

red tide: A brownish-red discoloration of marine waters caused by the presence of enormous numbers of certain microscopic flagellates that can produce a potent neurotoxin.

reef break: When waves break off a shallow coral or rock reef creating a hollow wave or barrel.

reform waves: Smaller waves that form after a large wave has broken and not lost its momentum.

reverse current: When current flows in different directions around an island or similar location.

rhomboids: Muscles associated with the shoulder blade that are primarily responsible for its retraction.

rip: Occurs when water escapes quickly in between sandbars on a beach, creating a flow or current like an underwater river.

river mouth: Where a river enters the ocean.

river signals: A standard method of communicating among paddlers using hand and arm signals.

rocker: Amount of curve from tail to nose of a board, as seen from the side of the board.

rooster tail: A spray of water above the surface created by river current colliding with a submerged rock.

rotator cuff: A group of four tendons that stabilize the shoulder joint, originating from the scapula.

rotomolded plastic: A thick durable plastic manufacturing technique used for many kayaks and boards.

SAM splint: A short rod or stick that can be used to stabilize a broken arm or leg.

sandbar: A sand mound in beaches and rivers that can affect wave types and sizes on the surface.

scapula: The bone that connects the humerus (arm bone) with the clavicle (collar bone). Also called shoulder blade.

scout: Getting off the board and going on shore to look around a blind corner on a river.

sculler: A single rower on a racing shell.

sculling brace: A method of placing the paddle flat and slightly submerged on the surface and rotating the wrist back and forth to help gain stability and support.

set: A group of ocean waves.

shaper: A person who carves a stand up paddleboard shape out of a block of foam and applies fiberglass and epoxy to finish the board.

shipping lane: An established route traversed by ocean shipping.

shore break: Where waves break close to shore in shallow water.

shoulder: The green unbroken section of a wave.

shuttle: When paddlers leave one car at the end of a river or downwind run, and have another car at the top of the run.

side draw: A paddle movement that pulls the board sideways.

sieve: Similar to a strainer, an obstruction in a river that allows only water to pass through it.

skeg: A fin or rudder that is attached or can be lowered below a boat or board and used for forward directional control or balance.

Skook: Nickname for large standing tidal rapid called Skookumchuk near Sechelt in British Columbia, Canada.

skull cap: A neoprene cap that covers your head and ears, used to stay warm in cold temperatures or while surfing.

slack: An unsettled or calm period between ebb and flood tides.

snag: A log or branch in the river that can snag or catch a paddler.

southerlies: Wind generated from the south.

southwesterly: Winds from the southwest.

standing wave: A surfable wave that stays in one place. Standing waves are found on rivers, tidal rapids, and tide rips.

starboard: Right side of a watercraft, when facing the front, or bow.

Steamer Lane: A famous surfing wave in Santa Cruz, CA known for its large waves and long rides.

stoke: Term used to described excitement or passion about surfing and paddling.

stopper: A hole or hydraulic in rivers.

strainer: An obstruction, such as a tree, in a river that lets only water pass through, trapping floating objects, including paddlers.

stringer: Strip of strengthening material (often wood) that runs the whole length of a foam board.

SUB: Stand up board, optional term for SUP.

sub-acromial bursa: A sac containing a small amount of lubricating fluid that lies under the roof of the shoulder and can develop into shoulder bursitis.

SUP: Stand up paddleboard.

supraspinatus muscle: Muscle located at the top of the shoulder joint. Its purpose is to help stabilize the shoulder joint and initiate raising the upper arm and moving it away from the body.

surf ski: A long sit-on-top kayak used for racing. Surf skis are very light and fast, and up to 22 feet long.

surfer's ear: A condition caused by excessive cold water in the ear, causing pain and irritation. Also known as exostosis.

swallow tail: A tail shape similar to a flat fish tail.

sweep stroke: A common kayaking stroke used in stand up paddling to turn the board by paddling on one side of the board.

sweeper: Overhanging rock or ledge with water flowing underneath.

swell: Storm-generated waves that travel long distances.

swift water rescue training: A subset of technical rescue that involves the use of specially trained personnel, ropes, and mechanical advantage systems. Also called "whitewater rescue."

Tahitian stroke: A short, quick forward stroke that is often used in racing, as it can move the board quickly.

tail: Back end of board.

tail rudder: A method commonly used with canoes, outriggers and kayaks that turns the board and aids in forward tracking, by placing the paddle by the tail while the board is moving.

take-out: Place where a trip is ended.

tendonitis: An inflammation of the tendon that occurs when the normal smooth gliding motion of the tendon is impaired so that it becomes inflamed and movement painful, commonly caused by overuse.

teres major: Muscle that helps in rotation of the arm.

teres minor muscle: One of the muscles that externally rotates the shoulder, found in the back of the shoulder joint.

throw bag: Bag that holds a long coiled rope, used in rescuing swimmers.

tidal current chart: Map of an area showing the direction of the currents through inlets and around islands at either ebb or flood. Some tidal charts list the minimum and maximum current in any certain area for daily tidal exchanges.

tidal exchange: The movement of water during the ebb or flood.

tidal rapids: Riverlike rapids created in narrow passageways where strong tidal exchanges occur.

tide: Alternate rising and falling of the surface of the ocean and of connected bodies of water that occurs twice a day as a result of differing gravitational forces exerted at different parts of the earth by another body (i.e. the moon or sun).

tide rip: Results when current in saltwater collides with an undersea obstruction forcing water to the surface, creating sections of rough water and often standing waves.

tide table: Shows hourly changes in tidal heights.

tiller: The skeg or rudder on a sailboat or sailboard.

tongue: The fastest, green water, flowing section of a river in between rapids. Also called a downstream V.

transverse abdominis: Deepest muscle of the abdominal muscles; it wraps around the spine for stability and protection and makes up part of the core.

trapezius: Muscle that moves the shoulder blade.

triceps: Arm muscle that extends or straightens the arm.

trough: The lower section in between two waves.

tube: Hollow section of a barreling wave where surfers like to surf. Also called the "green room."

undercut: Overhanging rock or ledge with water flowing underneath.

upstream: Direction opposite of the river flow.

USGS: United States Geological Survey; source for maps.

V-bottom: V-shaped bottoms on boards create more stability and make the board easier to turn.

VHF radio: Very High Frequency radio; band of radio frequencies falling between 30 and 300 megahertz. Channel 16 (156.8 MHz) is the international calling and distress channel.

volume: Measure of water in a river in cubic feet or cubic meters.

wall: Face of a wave.

waterfall: Large vertical drop.

wave: Where water falls over itself; created by wind, current, tides, a drop in elevation in rivers, and a decrease in space for an ocean wave to go.

wave train: Series of standing waves.

wet suit: A neoprene garment designed to keep a paddler or surfer warm when immersed in cold water.

white water: Aerated water created by breaking waves.

whitecaps: Wind-generated breaking waves.

wipeout: Falling off the board when surfing or paddling.

wood: A term used in river paddling to describe logs or strainers in a river.

Z-drag system: A pulley system used to rescue pinned kayakers; can also be used for rescuing swimmers on rivers.

RESOURCES

GENERAL

My Local Line Up, www.mylocallineup.com
Salmon Bay Paddle,
   www.salmonbaypaddle.com
   (Check here for instructional videos,
   additional photos and updates on mate-
   rial in this book.)
Stand Up Journal,
   www.standupjournal.com
Stand Up Paddle Magazine,
   www.standuppaddlemagazine.com
Stand Up Paddlesurf Magazine (online),
   www.standuppaddlesurf.net
Stand Up Zone, www.standupzone.com
SUP Magazine, www.supthemag.com
SUP Surf Magazine (online),
   www.supsurfmag.com
Wavelength Magazine, BC,
   www.wavelengthmagazine.com
Beau Whitehead,
   http://paddlesurfnorthwest.blogspot.com

EXPEDITIONS, NAVIGATION, AND SAFETY

Alderson, Doug. *The Savvy Paddler*.
   Camden, ME: McGraw Hill, 2001
Burch, David. *Fundamentals of Kayak
   Navigation,* 4th edition, Guilford, CT:
   Falcon Books / Globe Pequot Press, 2008.
Burch, David. *Modern Marine Weather*.
   Seattle: Starpath Publications, 2008.
Burns, Bob and Mike Burns. *Wilderness
   Navigation*, 2nd edition. Seattle:
   The Mountaineers Books, 2004.
Dowd, John. *Sea Kayaking, A Manual for
   Long Distance Touring*. Vancouver, BC:
   Greystone Books, 2004.
Hutchinson, Derek C. *Expedition Kayaking,*
   5th Edition. Guilford, CT: Globe Pequot,
   1999.
Lull, John. *Sea Kayaking Safety & Rescue*.
   Berkeley, CA: Wilderness Press,
   2002.

Heather Nelson after her heat in an open coastal SUP race

Moyer, Lee. *Sea Kayak Navigation Simplified*, Mukilteo, WA: Alpenbooks, 2001.

Stuhaug, Dennis O. *The Complete Idiot's Guide to Canoeing and Kayaking.* New York: Alpha Books, 2004.

White, Charlie. *Living Off the Sea.* Surrey, BC: Heritage House, 2010.

Marine Weather Service Charts, www.nws.noaa.gov/om/marine/pub.htm

NOAA Marine Chart Viewer, www.nauticalcharts.noaa.gov/mcd/OnLineViewer.html

Starpath School of Navigation, www.starpath.com

Surf Etiquette, www.asudoit.com/kayak_fest/surf_etiquette.html

US Boating Safety Resource Center, www.uscgboating.org

US Coast Guard Navigational Center, www.navcen.uscg.gov/pubs/LightLists/LightLists.htm

Washburne, Randel. *The Coastal Kayaker's Manual,* 3rd edition. Guilford, CT: Globe Pequot Press, 1998.

FISHING

BoardFisher Products, LLC, www.boardfisher.com

Null, Scott and Joel McBride. *Kayak Fishing, The Ultimate Guide.* Beachburg, Ontario: The Heliconia Press, 2008.

FITNESS

Nikki Gregg, http://nikkigregg.com

GEAR

Imagine Surfboards, www.imaginesurfboards.com

Infinity Surfboards, www.infinitysurf.com

Northwest Outdoor Center, Seattle, www.nwoc.com

Perfect Wave Surf Shop, www.perfectwave.com

Riviera Paddlesurf, www.rivierapaddlesurf.com

Starboard SUP, www.star-board-sup.com
Surf Ballard, Seattle, www.surfballard.com
Tomahawk Paddle Sports,
    www.tomahawksurf.com
Urban Surf, Seattle, www.urbansurf.com
Werner Paddles, www.wernerpaddles.com

INSTRUCTION AND GUIDING

Aspen Kayak Academy,
    www.riversup.com
Azimuth Expeditions, Tacoma, WA,
    www.lastwilderness.net/azimuth
    -expeditions
Dan Gavere, Professional Stand Up Paddler
    & Coach, www.supinstruction.com
*Mastering Stand Up Paddle Technique with
    Danny Chinn* (DVD),
    www.rivierapaddlesurf.com
Nikki Gregg, Fitness Professional & Professional Stand Up Paddler,
    http://nikkigregg.com
Lars L.E. Hansen, Professional
    Watermen, Instructor, & Santa Cruz
    Search & Rescue; Santa Cruz, CA &
    Oahu & Maui,
    www.surfinglessonssantacruz.com
Imagine Surfschool,
    www.imaginesurfboards.com
Dave Kalama, www.davidkalama.com
Leavenworth Mountain Sports,
    http://leavenworthmtnsports.com
Salmon Bay Paddle (author's site),
    www.salmonbaypaddle.com

MARINE TRAILS

American Trails, www.americantrails.org
The BC Marine Trails Network,
    www.bcmarinetrails.org
Washington Watertrails Association,
    www.wwta.org

RACING

Battle of the Paddle, www.rainbowsandals
    .com/battleofthepaddle
Deception Pass Dash, Anacortes, WA,
    www.deceptionpassdash.blogspot.com
Distressed Mullet,
    www.distressedmullet.com
Round the Rock, Mercer Island, WA,
    www.roundtherock.com
World Paddle Association,
    www.worldpaddleassociation.com

SURFING

Almond, Elliott. *Surfing: Mastering Waves
    from Basic to Intermediate.* Seattle: The
    Mountaineers Books, 2009.
Inland Surfer, www.inlandsurfer.com
Mattos, Bill. *Kayak Surfing,* Gwynedd,
    Wales: Pesda Press, 2004.
Santa Cruz Surf Kayak and SUP Festival,
    www.asudoit.com/kayak_fest
Werner, Doug. *Surfer's Start-Up.* Chula Vista,
    CA: Start-Up Sports / Tracks Publishing,
    2001.

WHITEWATER AND RIVERS

American Whitewater,
www.americanwhitewater.org
Bennett, Jeff. *The Essential Whitewater Kayaker*. Camden, ME: McGraw Hill, 1999.
USGS Water Resources of the United States,
http://water.usgs.gov
USGS River CFS Levels,
http://waterdata.usgs.gov/nwis
Whitewater Stand Up Paddling Championship, Glenwood Springs, Colorado,
www.whitewatersupchampionship.com

WEATHER AND TIDE INFORMATION

CANADA

Beaufort Wind Scale, www.spc.noaa.gov
/faq/tornado/beaufort.html
Canadian Hydrographic Service,
www.waterlevels.gc.ca
Weatheroffice: www.weatheroffice.gc.ca

USA

Golden, Frank and Michael Tipton, MD.
Essentials of Sea Survival. Champaign, IL: Human Kinetics, 2002.
Mobile Graphics, (tides),
www.mobilegeographics.com

National Weather Service,
www.nws.noaa.gov
NOAA Current Tables,
http://tidesandcurrents.noaa.gov
NOAA Marine Weather Forecast, www.nws
.noaa.gov/om/marine/zone/usamz.htm
NOAA, National Data Buoy Center,
www.ndbc.noaa.gov
NOAA Tide Tables,
http://tidesandcurrents.noaa.gov/
station_retrieve.shtml?type = Tide + Data
Saltwater Tides,
www.saltwatertides.com
USGS Maps, www.usgs.gov/pubprod

MISCELLANEOUS

Brewmug - http://brewmug.com
Dave Collins - www.tierralegre.org
Hamilton, Laird. *Force of Nature: Mind, Body, Soul and, Of Course, Surfing*. Emmaus, PA: Rodale Press, 2008.
Night Paddling Coast Guard Regulations,
www.olympicpeninsulapaddlers.com
/forms/OPP_NightPaddling.pdf
The Orca Network,
www.orcanetwork.org
Stand Up Zone,
www.standupzone.com
The Surfrider Foundation,
www.surfrider.org

Index

About the Author

A Seattle native, Rob Casey has been paddling sea and surf kayaks since the late 1990s. He first tried stand up paddling on a vacation to the Big Island in Hawaii in 2007. Intrigued by the simplicity of paddling a SUP, he began to see the versatility of paddling boards on various types of water. He paddles his SUP several days a week, but still finds time to kayak.

Rob has been a commercial and fine art photographer for twenty years and specializes in outdoor adventure and lifestyle images. His images are represented by Getty Images and Corbis. He has contributed his writing and images to numerous magazines including *Men's Journal, Canoe & Kayak,* and *Stand Up Paddle Journal*. He is the Northwest contributor to *SUP Magazine*

Rob teaches stand up paddling and kayaking through his business, Salmon Bay Paddle.

THE MOUNTAINEERS, founded in 1906, is a nonprofit outdoor activity and conservation organization based in Seattle, Washington. The Mountaineers' mission is "To enrich the community by helping people explore, conserve, learn about, and enjoy the lands and waters of the Pacific Northwest."

The Mountaineers sponsors classes and year-round outdoor activities, including hiking, mountain climbing, backpacking, skiing, snowboarding, snowshoeing, bicycling, camping, kayaking and canoeing, nature study, photography, sailing, and adventure travel; these classes and activities are open to both members and the general public. The Mountaineers conservation efforts support environmental causes through educational activities and programming, and through its publishing division. All activities are led by skilled, experienced volunteers, who are dedicated to promoting safe and responsible enjoyment and preservation of the outdoors. If you would like more information on programs or membership, please write to The Mountaineers Program Center, 7700 Sand Point Way NE, Seattle, WA 98115-3996; phone 206-521-6001; visit www.mountaineers.org; or e-mail clubmail@mountaineers.org.

The Mountaineers Books, the nonprofit publishing division of The Mountaineers, produces guidebooks, instructional texts, historical works, natural history guides, and, through partnership with Braided River, works on environmental conservation. Books are aimed at fulfilling the mission of The Mountaineers. For more information please visit www.mountaineersbooks.org and www.BraidedRiver.org.

The Mountaineers Books
1001 SW Klickitat Way, Suite 201
Seattle, WA 98134
800-553-4453
mbooks@mountaineersbooks.org
www.mountaineersbooks.org

The Mountaineers Books is proud to be a corporate sponsor of the Leave No Trace Center for Outdoor Ethics, whose mission is to promote and inspire responsible outdoor recreation through education, research, and partnerships. The Leave No Trace program is focused specifically on human-powered (nonmotorized) recreation. Leave No Trace strives to educate visitors about the nature of their recreational impacts, as well as offer techniques to prevent and minimize such impacts. Leave No Trace is best understood as an educational and ethical program, not as a set of rules and regulations.

For more information, visit www.lnt.org, or call 800-332-4100.

OTHER TITLES YOU MIGHT ENJOY FROM THE MOUNTAINEERS BOOKS

Chasing Waves: A Surfer's Tale of Obsessive Wandering
Amy Waeschle
The first travel-adventure book written by a female surfer

**SPIRITED WATERS
Soloing South Through the Inside Passage**
Jennifer Hahn
A gripping account of a challenging solo kayak journey

**SURFING
Mastering Waves from Basic to Intermediate**
Elliott Almond
A comprehensive and friendly guide to learning to surf

**THE ZEN OF OCEANS AND SURFING
Wit, Wisdom, and Inspiration**
Katharine Wroth, editor
foreword by Gerry Lopez
Inspirational quotes on all things oceanic